Carving

JAPANESE
NETSUKE

for Beginners

Carving
JAPANESE
NETSUKE
for Beginners

ROBERT JUBB

GUILD OF MASTER
CRAFTSMAN PUBLICATIONS

First published 2011 by
Guild of Master Craftsman Publications Ltd
Castle Place, 166 High Street, Lewes,
East Sussex BN7 1XU

Text © Robert Jubb, 2011

© in the Work GMC Publications Ltd, 2011
ISBN: 978-1-86108-693-8

A catalogue record for this book is available
from the British Library.

Publisher: Jonathan Bailey
Production Manager: Jim Bulley
Managing Editor: Gerrie Purcell
Editor: Beth Wicks
Managing Art Editor: Gilda Pacitti
Designer: Rob Janes
Photography: Robert Jubb and Anthony Bailey

Colour origination by GMC Reprographics
Printed and bound in China by Hing Yip
Printing Co. Ltd.

CONTENTS

Acknowledgements

Firstly, I would like to thank Sue Wraight, whose wonderful work first encouraged me to start carving netsuke and for her inspiration and support ever since. Sue has also kindly allowed me to include photographs of her fantastic work in this book.

My thanks also go to Dorothy and Paul, for allowing me to photograph their collections of netsuke and include them in this book. Both of you have been a great encouragement.

Helen, Bob and Pauline, thank you for returning netsuke pieces that I have carved for you for photography purposes.

I have also received much encouragement from my wife Julie, my family and my woodcarving friends while writing this book, especially Mick and Pat, who regularly enquired of its progress and encouraged me to continue with it.

Finally, I would like to thank Beth Wicks and Rob Janes of GMC Publications for all their hard work and editing/design skills.

INTRODUCTION

My interest in carving Japanese netsuke goes back a long way. I really enjoy learning about these miniature works of art, drawing them and carving them, usually with pleasing results. For many years, I travelled the world as part of my job, staying in hotels in the middle of nowhere with very little to do in the evenings. To keep myself busy, I would take a couple of netsuke and a few small tools with me and carve in my room. This was both relaxing and enjoyable, but I often wondered what the cleaners thought when they noticed the wood chippings in the waste bin.

I have read many books on the subject of netsuke, yet there are very few that explain how to carve one. Now that I'm retired, I have the time to pass on what I have learned and to attempt to fill this gap. I don't claim to have written the comprehensive manual on netsuke carving, but simply to have provided enough information to encourage carvers to give it a go.

Miniature carving is not as difficult as many people think. It does require mastering some small hand carving tools and larger power tools to cut in confined places, but otherwise the skills are very much the same as ordinary carving.

In this book, I explain what netsuke are, their practical purpose and the different types that can be found. I take you through six netsuke stage-by-stage to demonstrate the process and the specific carving and finishing techniques.

Throughout I use my own unique method, developed over a long period of time. This is not the traditional Japanese method which early Japanese netsuke carvers served a long apprenticeship to learn. Yet all methods work towards achieving the same result – a fine miniature netsuke carving.

This leads on to 23 netsuke carving projects. Each project starts with a detailed reference drawing and finishes with the carved piece viewed from every angle, providing all the information you need to carve the piece yourself.

The book finishes with a gallery section featuring more of my own work, pieces belonging to close friends and more importantly, pieces created by netsuke carver Sue Wraight. Some of these netsuke are old, some modern and some never shown in public before now.

WHAT ARE JAPANESE NETSUKE?

The traditional kimono worn by Japanese men between the sixteenth and nineteenth centuries had one drawback: the absence of pockets. Everyday items such as money, tobacco and medicine were therefore carried in small containers (*sagemono* or *inro*) which were hung by a cord from the sash (*obi*) of the kimono and held shut by the *ojime*.

The word *netsuke* is pronounced 'netske' with a silent 'u' and simply means 'root attach' as it would have originally been made from a tree root or a branch. Netsuke were designed to be a simple toggle that prevented the cord connected to the *sagemono* or *inro* from being pulled through the sash of the kimono.

Exactly when netsuke were first worn remains unknown, but it is generally accepted that they were in regular use from the early 1600s, although some people believe that it was much earlier. What is agreed on is that netsuke were created to serve a practical need in the everyday life of the Japanese people.

Netsuke

Ojime

Inro

A decorative *inro*.

In History

The following historical events acted as a stimulus for the introduction of netsuke. In 1542, Portuguese adventurers were the first Europeans to find their way to Japan. Among the things they introduced was tobacco, which quickly caught on among the working classes. Consequently, portable pipe cases, tobacco boxes, ash trays and fire lighters were soon in high demand and netsuke were rapidly created to ensure secure transportation.

In 1592, the Shogun Hideyoshi (The Japanese Commander-in-Chief) sent a large expeditionary force to conquer China and Korea. The plan failed and they returned six years later unvictorious but with many acquired artefacts and materials. The Japanese looked on these new items favourably and adopted several of them into their culture, including the custom of sealing documents. The necessary seals and ink were kept in the *inro* and the netsuke once more came into use.

After 450 years of civil war, peace descended upon Japan in 1603. Dutch merchants arrived around the same time. They were soon involved in petty jealousies with their Portuguese trade rivals which led to the expulsion of the Portuguese

The other side of the *inro*.

from Japan. In 1641, a small colony of the Dutch East India Company was given permission to establish itself, under strict surveillance, on the small island of Deshima in Nagasaki harbour and to continue to trade with the Japanese. A few privileged Chinese merchants were also allowed to trade there, but otherwise Japan closed its borders to international trade and the outside world for over 200 years.

1603 is also the year considered by many to mark the beginning of national art in Japan, with netsuke being just one of the many art forms which developed. The lengthy seclusion ensured that Japanese art developed with minimal, if any, external influence and with the encouragement of the ruling classes. As a result, all forms of art flourished and the most meticulous and beautiful work was created. Rich Japanese merchants, for example, would seek out any opportunity to display their wealth and would purchase netsuke intricately carved in wood, ivory, coral, antler, lacquer and many other semi-precious materials. These beautiful miniature carvings were generally between 1in (25mm) and 3¼in (80mm) in size and were expertly crafted.

For almost three hundred years, from the early 1600s to the late 1800s, netsuke became the main objects on which professional sculptors applied their skills. Japanese life in its entirety was represented in netsuke. Intricate scenes from everyday life, people, all kinds of animals, birds, fish and insects would be carved. Early carvers also created figures, ghosts, and sages taken from ancient Japanese stories or fables – some humorous and some frightening – or objects such as gourds, baskets, boxes and masks. Incredible detail and skill were put into these miniature

sculptures, with some of the best examples of netsuke believed to have taken over two months of painstaking work to create. The end products were inevitably outstanding and astonishing works of art. Over the years many netsuke have become polished through wear and handling, yet this simply adds to their beauty.

VARIOUS TYPES OF NETSUKE

Explaining the full range of netsuke is well beyond the scope of this book, but it is helpful to explore the main types of netsuke that have developed over the centuries. Here, photographs have also been used to clearly illustrate the main differences between the various types of netsuke.

Quite often, schools of netsuke carvers would concentrate on carving just one type of netsuke and the skills would be passed on from father to son. Other schools would concentrate on a particular subject, such as horses or tigers.

Katabori netsuke

The most common type of netsuke are *katabori*, literally meaning 'shape carving' or 'carved in the round'. These are miniature sculptures of real people, animals, birds and so on. Each one has two holes or a natural opening for the cord.

Many *katabori* netsuke are based on the Oriental signs of the zodiac which are illustrated on the following page. Some of the pieces demonstrate traditional Japanese design, while others are modern ones which I have designed and carved myself. As you go through books and Internet pages on netsuke you will see these particular animals time and time again.

Pig with piglet and bag on its back.

Toad carved in buffalo horn.

Tagua nut walrus.

Rooster in wood.

Ox in boxwood.

Tiger carved in ivory.

Rat carved in wood.

Goat in boxwood.

Boar carved in ivory.

Hare carved in wood.

Snake encoiling a toad in boxwood.

Horse carved in ivory.

Monkey carved in wood.

Dragon inlaid with paua shell.

Dog carved in wood.

Manju netsuke

Another very popular type is *manju* netsuke. These are designed in a flat cake shape which resemble a round Japanese dumpling, although they may also be oval or square. The majority of manju netsuke are solid, but occasionally they come in two parts. They have holes on the back or a ring to accept the cord. *Ryusa* netsuke are a variety of *manju* pieces with flowers, birds or other carvings on the surface which are pierced through to the back.

Kagami netsuke

Kagami netsuke (also referred to as *kagamibuta*) are small bowls, usually made from ivory or wood, into which a metal disc fits. Sometimes this disc is a mirror, or it is elaborately decorated with all kinds of different subjects, including birds and flowers or humorous subjects. The bowl has a central hole through which the cord passes and connects to a ring on the back of the disc.

Comic mask in boxwood.

Mask netsuke

These *mask* netsuke are miniature masks of the kind which were once used in Japanese theatre. Many of these are humorous, some are frightening. Each one has a horizontal bar at the back for attaching the cord.

Additional netsuke

Other types of netsuke are less common and in some cases quite rare. These include *ichiraku* netsuke – usually gourd-shaped and made from woven bamboo, wire or cane; *hako* netsuke – small boxes; *kagebori* netsuke – carvings of baskets or cages; *kurumiki* – hollowed and perforated netsuke like figures in a clam shell; and *shikakemono* or trick netsuke – with hidden movable parts, such as levers, which move parts such as protruding tongues and eyes. (At the time of writing, I am working on a beetle netsuke which has a small pendulum in it and will flip up its wings when tilted, to reveal a mother of pearl underwing). Finally, *sashi* netsuke – this lies between the sash and the kimono, with only the top part that hooks over the sash visible. These are very rare.

Manju dragon in boxwood.

Kagami butterfly inlaid in African blackwood.

Tools & Equipment

THE TOOLBOX

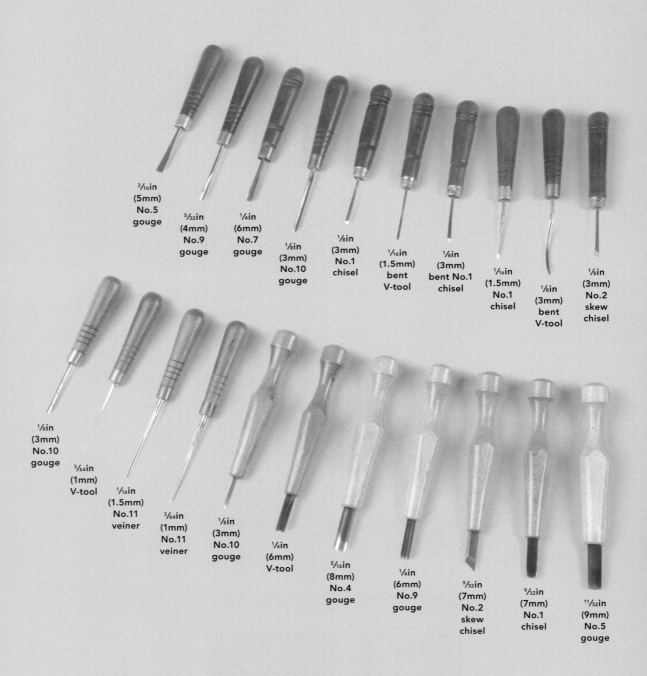

³⁄₁₆in (5mm) No.5 gouge

⁵⁄₃₂in (4mm) No.9 gouge

¼in (6mm) No.7 gouge

⅛in (3mm) No.10 gouge

⅛in (3mm) No.1 chisel

¹⁄₁₆in (1.5mm) bent V-tool

⅛in (3mm) bent No.1 chisel

¹⁄₁₆in (1.5mm) No.1 chisel

⅛in (3mm) bent V-tool

⅛in (3mm) No.2 skew chisel

⅛in (3mm) No.10 gouge

³⁄₆₄in (1mm) V-tool

¹⁄₁₆in (1.5mm) No.11 veiner

³⁄₆₄in (1mm) No.11 veiner

⅛in (3mm) No.10 gouge

¼in (6mm) V-tool

⁵⁄₁₆in (8mm) No.4 gouge

¼in (6mm) No.9 gouge

⁹⁄₃₂in (7mm) No.2 skew chisel

⁹⁄₃₂in (7mm) No.1 chisel

¹¹⁄₃₂in (9mm) No.5 gouge

The tools I have assembled over the years for carving netsuke are shown in the photographs below. I have bought some, made some, and modified others. A friend of mine made some matching handles for many of them so that they look as though they are part of a set.

Don't be put off by the number of tools shown here. You only need a small selection to start with. For the most part, I regularly use a small number of the same tools for most of my carvings, using the other tools for special techniques or for solving particular problems.

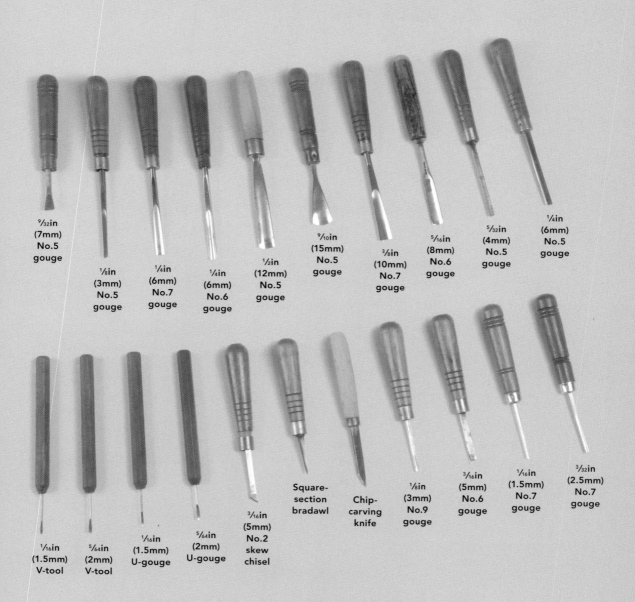

9/32in (7mm) No.5 gouge

1/8in (3mm) No.5 gouge

1/4in (6mm) No.7 gouge

1/4in (6mm) No.6 gouge

1/2in (12mm) No.5 gouge

9/10in (15mm) No.5 gouge

3/8in (10mm) No.7 gouge

5/16in (8mm) No.6 gouge

5/32in (4mm) No.5 gouge

1/4in (6mm) No.5 gouge

1/16in (1.5mm) V-tool

5/64in (2mm) V-tool

1/16in (1.5mm) U-gouge

5/64in (2mm) U-gouge

3/16in (5mm) No.2 skew chisel

Square-section bradawl

Chip-carving knife

1/8in (3mm) No.9 gouge

3/16in (5mm) No.6 gouge

1/16in (1.5mm) No.7 gouge

3/32in (2.5mm) No.7 gouge

Shaping Tools

In addition to the carving tools shown on the previous pages, there are several other tools used for carving netsuke. They are all readily available and only the *ukibori* tool had to be specially made, although this is not an essential tool for getting started.

Cutting Tools

Bandsaw

When cutting out the netsuke profile in side elevation and plan view, a bandsaw makes easy work of preparing the wood. I almost always cut out two netsuke at a time, by holding one end while cutting the other end. I then change it around so that my hands are further away from the blade. If you have never used a bandsaw, perhaps you should get some lessons first.

A word of warning though; because netsuke are so small, your hands will be very near the cutting edge of the bandsaw blade. Keep your hands to the side or behind the blade, never immediately in front. Another rule I always stick to is never to use the bandsaw if anyone else is in the workshop. It needs 100 per cent concentration – just one second of distraction can result in a serious injury.

A bandsaw for preparation work.

Coping saw

This will give you much the same results as a bandsaw, yet for the finer cutting it is best to use a coping saw. Although it will take you a little longer, it is not a significant amount of extra time. You can also obtain different sized blades for your coping saw; use the thick blade to create straight cuts or the thin one to create complicated shapes.

Coping saw for finer cuts.

Fret saw

This is a useful tool for accurately cutting out the complicated shapes so often associated with netsuke. A fret saw has a fine blade with an up-and-down cutting motion, and will cut wood of up to 1½in (40mm) thick very accurately. They are also referred to as scrollsaws and can be machine or hand-driven.

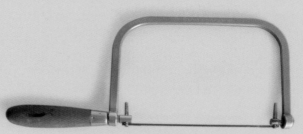
Different sized blades for the coping saw.

Sanding wheel

In my workshop, I have a vertically mounted drill with a sanding disc on top which I use for roughly rounding off and shaping pieces before the detailed carving starts. The disc is Velcro-backed for easy changing to different grades of sandpaper. This is a very useful piece of equipment, especially when rounding off square pieces of wood or buffalo horn to make circular or oval cross-section eyes.

Sanding wheel with discs.

Fret saws cut accurately.

Woodcarving tools

The carving tools I have bought or modified over the years are a motley collection of tools which cater for almost all aspects of netsuke carving. If I come across a problem that I cannot sort out with my existing tools, I will make or amend an existing tool. It is not necessary to have all these tools when starting out. I only use a small number of them on a regular basis; the others come into play only when I encounter specific problems or need them for difficult areas. You will no doubt acquire further tools as time goes on, so that you can achieve specific tasks.

The boxes I use to carry these tools around in are modified artists' paint boxes, see below. They are inexpensive and very handy for moving your tools around with ease.

Only by putting them to use can we see how each of the various gouges and chisels handle and what can be achieved with them. As we are working on miniature carvings, there is no need to remove large quantities of wood. The gouges and chisels will therefore be small and require hand pressure rather than a mallet. Generally, flatter gouges are used for removing thin chips of wood, while the deeper gouges remove thicker chips of wood. The width of the tool will determine the width of the chip.

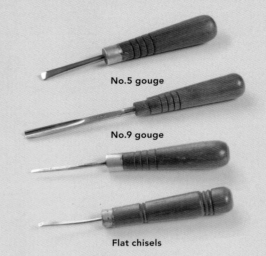

No.5 gouge

No.9 gouge

Flat chisels

No.5 gouge

The ³⁄₁₆in (5mm) No.5 gouge is one of my most frequently used gouges for carving the general shape of a netsuke. It removes thin chips and enables you to carve down to a line without accidently overdoing it.

No.9 gouge

The slightly larger ¼in (6mm) No.9 gouge is used to remove larger chips of wood, to define features on a netsuke, and to remove wood quickly from alongside such features. For example, let's say that you are carving the side of a frog or a rabbit. Once the edges of the legs have been marked in with this gouge, you can cut down to the body level between the front and back legs with it. Be careful not to cut too deeply when getting down to a drawn outline, as it is quite easy to go over the line with this gouge.

Flat chisels

I frequently use flat chisels in various widths to pare down the outside of a curved surface or to clean up to a line. By using a ¹⁄₁₆in (1.5mm) chisel you are able to get into all kinds of difficult places to clean out loose woodchips. Skew or angled flat chisels are also useful for cutting into tight corners.

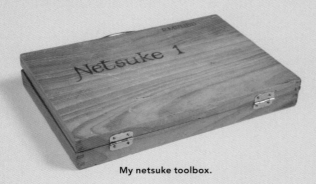

My netsuke toolbox.

V-tool

The 1/16in (1.5mm) V-tool is almost exclusively used for carving hair, outlining features such as tails or legs, or for long cuts on snail shells and such like. These small tools can be obtained from several manufacturers, some of which specialize in V-tools and U-gouges going down to 1/16in (1.5mm) wide. Good tools remain sharp for a long time and, if they are used and put away properly, will last for ages. I keep one solely for carving hair, which means the cuts are consistently sharp.

U-tool

The 1/16in (1.5mm) u-gouge is ideal for outlining features such as eyebrows, ears, limbs and tails, as the cut does not need to be sharply defined.

Curved-shaft tools

Gouges and chisels with curved shafts are useful for cutting in inaccessible areas where a straight shaft does not present the cutting edge at the right angle to the wood. These small tools are best held like a pencil, between your thumb and the next two fingers; this makes carving more comfortable.

Most of the other tools used in netsuke carving are variations of those already mentioned. With experience and time you will get to know which ones are the best to work with.

Additional tools

Callipers

Small callipers are useful for checking dimensions on a carving against the drawing. They should be used regularly to keep the main features of the netsuke in the right place as the carving proceeds.

Scrapers

Various scrapers are used to clean and smooth the surface of a netsuke, as well as getting into small confined areas where sandpapers cannot reach. These scrapers can produce a really smooth finish and, in my view, are a much under-rated tool. They all need to have a really sharp edge, but their shapes can vary considerably, depending on what they are required to do.

Bradawl

'Sparrow pecking' requires a bradawl to be pushed into the wood several times in close proximity so that it marks the wood with indentations. The overall effect is to make the background appear to recede while the foreground stands out further. It is a technique often used to make bumps stand out on a toad netsuke. The bradawl can be either square in cross-section or round, making the marks on the wood slightly, but perceptibly different.

The flat scraper.

An assortment of callipers.

The round-section and square-section bradawls.

Ukibori tool

Ukibori is a unique Japanese technique used to make small bumps on a wooden surface. A round-ended ball is pressed into the surface of the wood, then gouges are used to carve down to the bottom of the depressions. Finally, warm water is placed on the surface so that these marks swell up to produce bumps. I created my own tool for this purpose using a large nail. I filed the end to a round shape, hardened it to a straw colour on the gas burner, then quenched it in water to harden it. I added a large-diameter handle to it so that it could be held easily in the palm of my hand and maximum pressure applied to the surface of the wood.

Files

I use many different files when making netsuke, all of which are differentiated by their coarseness. Ultimately, no scratch marks should remain on the surface of the carving, so the larger areas of wood are removed with a coarse file, followed by finer files and finally sandpaper. For small localized areas you can use fine files from the outset. Below is a selection of files that I use. The file on the end of the Sandvik sanding plate is replaceable with a self-adhesive plate. This is very good for shaping larger areas. The small diamond files and various needle files are all very useful for getting into confined spaces. The final picture shows Perma-Grit tungsten carbide files with different shapes at each end.

Modified *ukibori* tool.

A Sandvik sanding plate.

Small diamond files.

Various-shaped needle files.

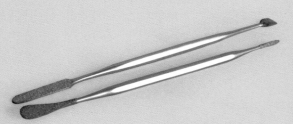

Perma-Grit tungsten carbide files.

Sandpaper and sanding sticks

There are numerous types of sandpaper, all graded in grit size. The lower the number the coarser the grit is and, conversely, the higher the number the finer the grit. Netsuke carving only requires fine-grit sandpaper. I usually start off using 120 grit and progress to around 400. Each time you progress to a higher grade of sandpaper you are aiming to remove the scratches made by the previous grade of sandpaper. In my opinion, the best sandpaper to use on miniature carvings is a flexible one with a cloth backing that can be folded and used in confined areas.

Sanding sticks can often be useful for getting into particularly awkward places. If an area of sandpaper becomes worn, the band of sandpaper can be moved along to an unused bit of paper or the sandpaper bands replaced if necessary. Having said this, the grades of paper that can be used are limited.

Micro-Mesh paper and sticks

Micro-Mesh paper was a fantastic find. It was first developed for polishing gems, but it also works very well on wood. The grit size goes up to an unbelievable 12,000 which gives wood an amazing shine. 4-way buffer and sanding sticks by Micro-Mesh have four grades on the same stick, two on each side. The coarsest is black, followed by the pink, then the white and finally the finest, grey. They are excellent tools for finishing the surface of a netsuke before polishing.

Pencils

Do not overlook the lowly pencil; it is a major part of drawing your design on the wood. If the pencil lead is too soft, for example a 2B, the lines will simply rub off as you carve. Therefore, I suggest using an H or 2H. If you are working with a dark wood, draw with a white-leaded pencil, so that you can see the lines clearly. Avoid using felt-tips as the ink bleeds into the wood and then has to be removed. I use a fine-tipped black ink pen because the lines are very fine and the ink barely penetrates the surface of the wood so marks can be scratched off easily with a scraper.

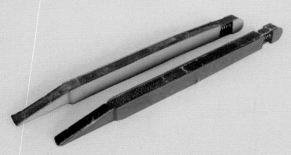

Sanding sticks with different grades of sandpaper.

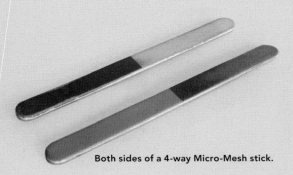

Both sides of a 4-way Micro-Mesh stick.

A selection of pencils.

ROTARY POWER TOOLS

Over the years, I have acquired several burrs and cutters for use in rotary machines, which have all been useful additions for carving netsuke. There are many different models available to suit all requirements and budgets.

The first machine I used was a small and light Minicraft. This was fantastic for getting into awkward places which seemed inaccessible. The multi-tool which followed was much heavier, but also much more powerful, with adjustable speed settings. Since then, many similar makes and many more powerful and lighter machines have come onto the market, including flexible-drive machines. They all have a range of collets to accommodate different cutter shaft diameters. A word of caution: although they appear to cut down costs, I've found that many of the cheaper models are less reliable in the long run and often have to be replaced relatively quickly.

It is important to be aware that power tools create a lot of dust, so, at the very least, ensure that you use a mask to protect your lungs and, ideally, a dust extractor.

The light weight Minicraft drill.

The multi-tool and other rotary machines.

Below are the cutters used for carving netsuke. They are shown in groups with diameters and descriptions beneath.

There are, of course, many others and you will soon get to know which ones best meet your requirements.

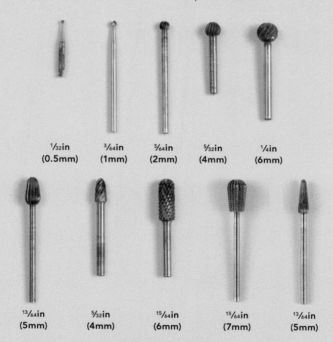

| $\frac{1}{32}$in (0.5mm) | $\frac{3}{64}$in (1mm) | $\frac{5}{64}$in (2mm) | $\frac{5}{32}$in (4mm) | $\frac{1}{4}$in (6mm) |

| $\frac{13}{64}$in (5mm) | $\frac{5}{32}$in (4mm) | $\frac{15}{64}$in (6mm) | $\frac{15}{64}$in (7mm) | $\frac{13}{64}$in (5mm) |

Top row: Round-ended cutters. Bottom row: Waste-removing cutters.

Round-ended cutters are used for drilling eyes and cord holes and for carving around bumps. They are also used for general shaping and removal of wood in confined spaces where the grain and the angle of access do not permit carving gouges to cut properly.

Waste-removing cutters remove waste wood on the outside of a carving. For example, after the outline of a netsuke has been cut out on the bandsaw in both directions (elevation and plan), I often use one of these cutters to round off the corners, then rough out the overall shape of the netsuke, before adding the details.

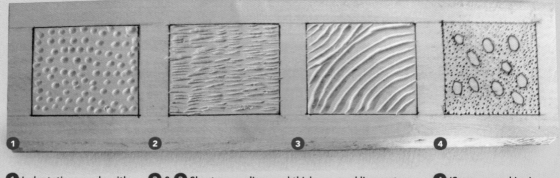

1 Indentations made with round-ended cutters.

2 & **3** Short coarse lines and thicker curved lines cut with inverted-cone cutters.

4 'Sparrow pecking' with conical cutters.

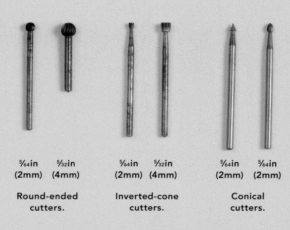

⁵⁄₆₄in (2mm)   ⁵⁄₃₂in (4mm)

Round-ended cutters.

⁵⁄₆₄in (2mm)   ⁵⁄₃₂in (4mm)

Inverted-cone cutters.

⁵⁄₆₄in (2mm)   ⁵⁄₆₄in (2mm)

Conical cutters.

In the sample panel above, I have shown the various textures which can be created using the different cutters in the multi-tool.

Starting from the left, the indentations are made with round-ended cutters **1**. This particular texture is effectively used in traditional netsuke carvings of frogs and toads.

Used on their edge, inverted-cone cutters can be used to cut rough lines **2** **3**. Here, they have been used to carve both short and thicker, longer hair. I have used these cutters successfully to carve the hair on several mice and to create the scales on tortoise shells.

The two conical cutters on the right are used for 'sparrow pecking' **4**, and for drilling nostrils in frogs and toads. With the drill running, the cutters are pressed into the surface to make neat little holes. The depth can be varied to change the size of the holes.

It is easy to make a mistake using these cutters as they are rotating so fast, so practice on spare pieces of wood before using them on the netsuke.

Power carving has sped up the process of netsuke carving quite considerably. The main advantage is that you can get down to a roughed -out shape relatively quickly, giving you more time to focus on adding the details with your conventional carving tools.

MATERIALS

Early Japanese netsuke carvers would use all suitable available materials, both local and imported, to make these intricate, miniature sculptures. The most common materials were wood and ivory, but many other materials were used to good effect.

Wood

The native woods most frequently used were Japanese cypress, yew, camellia, cherry and boxwood. Other types of timber, such as ebony, persimmon, and sandalwood, were imported probably for furniture or to create other larger wooden objects. Any offcuts were used to make netsuke. The main requirement was that the wood should be durable. If it had an unusual colour – for example, ebony – or smell – for example, sandalwood, that was an added bonus.

I can just imagine the excitement of Japanese netsuke carvers when a new material arrived from overseas, opening up many new possibilities.

Ivory

All ivory tusks and spikes are the extended teeth of one animal or another. Elephant ivory is not indigenous to Japan, so tusks from Indian elephants were imported through China, mostly from Asian countries. African elephant tusks were also used for netsuke when Japan finally opened its borders

to international trade, and materials from all over the world became available. Walrus tusk and narwhal spikes were also imported into Japan for the creation of netsuke. Wild boar, on the other hand, are indigenous to Japan and their tusks, particularly those of the male whose tusks are longer, were used for carving netsuke. Marine ivory, in the form of whales' teeth, would have also been available for use.

Other materials

Other materials that were traditionally used include deer antler, coral and amber. Netsuke were even cast in metal or made from fired porcelain. Lacquer was also used and was built up in layers before being carved. Many of these traditional materials are still available in addition to the more modern materials used today.

On the following pages, I have described the materials that I have used in carving netsuke, as well as some that I have acquired and intend to use in the future.

Wood

Boxwood (*Buxus sempervirens*)

My favourite wood for carving netsuke is boxwood. It is very slow-growing and therefore close-grained and very strong, enabling detailed carving in any direction. Boxwood is hard to carve, but very rewarding. When freshly cut, its colour is creamy yellow. This gradually goes darker with age to become a rich honey colour. It is relatively easily obtained from timber companies who supply carving materials and turning blocks.

Holly (*Ilex aquifolium*)

This is a close-grained, whitish-grey wood that takes good detail and carves well. The grain is not predominant, other than a little speckling in the wood which does not detract from the carving.

Pearwood (*Pyrus communis*)

This is a uniform rich brown wood that takes good detail and polishes well. Again the grain does not predominate, so the detailed carving is not spoiled by grain effects.

Lime (*Tilia spp*)

A whitish wood that carves easily, but occasionally does not take fine detail, for example, when carving hair. Therefore, I prefer to carve smooth-surface netsuke in this wood. With age, lime goes a honey colour. It polishes up well.

Boxwood octopus.

Pearwood baby rat.

Holly rabbit.

Sleeping wild boar in lime.

Cherry (*Prunus spp*)

Another lovely wood with which to carve. Cherry wood is a nice golden colour and polishes well. However, often pieces have a strong grain, so the subject has to be carefully chosen.

African blackwood (*Dalbergia melanoxylon*)

This is a lovely uniformly black wood. It is hard to carve, but well worth the effort as the finished netsuke looks exceptional and takes on a lovely shine. Blackwood is readily available from suppliers of exotic timber.

Pink ivory wood (*Berchemia zeyheri*)

This is an endangered species from South Africa where felling of these trees is strictly controlled. The wood is very hard to carve but, like boxwood, takes very high detail and shines well. Its pink colour gradually turns darker with time.

Huon pine (*Lagarostrobos franklinii*)

This particular wood comes from Tasmania and is another endangered species, yet limited quantities are available. Most other pines are difficult to carve because of the different layers of soft and hard wood, and they do not polish up well. In contrast, Huon pine is much easier to carve, will take a good polish and also gives off a lovely smell when worked.

Bat in cherry.

Pink ivory snail.

African blackwood mole.

Huon pine toadstools.

Ivory

Elephant ivory

Although the buying and selling of new elephant ivory has now been banned worldwide, ivory can still be obtained from pre-1925 billiard balls and other second-hand ivory objects. Recycling the ivory and using it to carve netsuke for your own collection is a way of putting this material to good use. Elephant ivory has a distinct grain which makes it easily differentiated from other types of ivory, tagua nut or plastic copies.

Other sources of ivory

Professional netsuke carvers in the Far East replaced elephant ivory with mammoth tusks. The majority of mammoth ivory comes from Russia. Whales' teeth are another, if unlikely, source of ivory. Inuits and sailors on old whaling ships used to carve and engrave whales' teeth; the latter was referred to as 'scrimshaw'. Wild boar tusk is also a source of ivory. I obtained several small pieces whilst on a business trip to Namibia.

Imitation ivory

A type of plastic ivory, referred to as imitation ivory, is also available. It cuts and files easily and polishes well. I haven't made a complete netsuke out of this material yet, but I have used it for inlaying eyes in toads, for example.

Tagua nut

These nuts are often referred to as 'vegetable ivory', because they are very hard to carve and look similar to ivory. They come from the palm tree *Phytelephas macrocarpa*, a member of the family of 'ivory palms' that grow on both sides of the South American Andes. The Indians in this area of the world regard tagua as a special carving material. In Japan, it is referred to as *bunroji* and has been used for over a hundred years. Tagua nuts are non-toxic and are often stained by soaking them in black tea to take on a mellow look. They are also readily available from suppliers of exotic timbers.

A piece of imitation ivory.

Boar tusk (left), whale's tooth (back), and elephant ivory in the form of a billiard ball (right).

Uncarved tagua nuts.

Other materials

Amber and Copal

Amber is expensive to buy in any amount suitable for carving. I have carved one piece in amber, a snake. I have also used amber to inlay the eyes in netsuke carp and toads. Recently, I came across a material called copal, which is sold as 'young amber'. This is obviously a pine tree resin, just like amber, with similar colours – from pale yellow to orange – and with insects encapsulated in it. It is much cheaper than amber, so I have already purchased some to carve in the future.

Deer antler

Some netsuke carvers also use deer horn. As many UK stickmakers use this material, it is readily available from firms who specialize in stickmaking. I have recently acquired some, but have not yet carved it.

Snake partially carved in amber.

Tagua nut snail.

The shape of this piece of copal already suggests an octopus.

Tagua nut polar bear made in China.

Deer antler.

Buffalo horn

Uniformly black and dense, buffalo horn can also be purchased from stickmaking firms. It is fairly hard to carve, yet it saws and files easily and carves well with woodcarving chisels, albeit with small cuts. It also takes on an incredible shine. I have already carved a stylized crow in buffalo horn, shown below. A mole is next on my list for a future netsuke as this would be an excellent subject to carve from this material.

Soapstone

This is another material that is readily available, this time in the form of a variety of carved objects originating from Africa. Soapstone is easy to carve using woodcarving chisels, it takes very fine detail and polishes well. However, the hardness of soapstone varies considerably and occasionally stonecarving chisels and rasps are needed to work it. It also comes in a wide variety of colours. I have both pinky-white and pale green soapstone.

Malachite

Malachite and other stones are carvable, but with much more difficulty as they tend to be a lot harder. Although it took a lot of effort to carve the malachite frog shown below, it was worthwhile as the malachite gave it a superb green colour. Malachite is available from stone and fossil shops.

A piece of buffalo horn.

Stylized crow in buffalo horn.

Malachite egg bought in Namibia.

Uncut green soapstone and partly carved rabbit in pink soapstone.

Malachite frog netsuke.

Inserts and inlays

I use various materials for inlaying eyes, such as ivory or imitation ivory, buffalo horn, amber, and other semi-precious stones. Shiny black buffalo horn is ideal for birds' eyes or for toad's pupils. I have also tried different-coloured woods for inlaying eyes, for example using holly for the iris and African blackwood for the pupil. The colour of the iris is only limited to the different colours of wood that are available.

Paua shell is a great material to use for creating scales, for example on a dragon netsuke, while mother of pearl is excellent for insects, such as a beetle's underwing. These are all readily available from fossil or stone shops. There are also coloured imitation resins that can be used to imitate these materials. It is also possible to inlay with wood veneers for surface effects such as scales.

I hope that this has given you an idea of the materials that were used by the early netsuke carvers and those that are available today. There are many additional materials that could be used and I'm sure that once you have made one or two netsuke, you will start experimenting with other woods and materials to achieve unique designs.

Sticks of various resins.

Shells for mother of pearl.

Paua shell, mother of pearl, amber, and different-coloured stones.

SAFETY

Like all types of woodcarving, there are hazards in carving netsuke, often more so because of their small size and the closeness of your fingers to cutting edges. With a bit of forethought, these issues can be managed quite easily. Make a habit of thinking about what you will be doing next and how you can do it safely. The quickest way to do something is not always the safest.

Sawing

Hand sawing with a fret saw or a coping saw is generally quite safe. It is the machine-driven saws, such as the bandsaw and fret saw, which need to be treated with the greatest respect. When you are cutting out the profile of a netsuke with a machine-driven saw, keep your fingers to the side or behind the cutting edge of the blade.

Carving

When you are holding a netsuke in your hand to carve, it is almost impossible to keep both hands behind the cutting edge of the carving tool. Carving gloves will protect the hand that is holding the work from the occasional slip, so shop around to see what is available and which one suits you best.

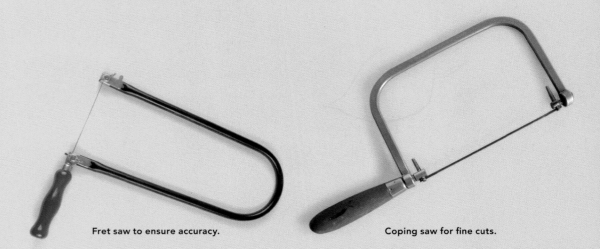

Fret saw to ensure accuracy.

Coping saw for fine cuts.

As you will see from the carving process explained later in this book, I often carve two netsuke back to back with a small central block in between, so I can hold one end while carving the other. If one netsuke is carved on its own, I leave a small block of wood to one side of the netsuke to hold it while carving. This keeps the hand holding the netsuke away from the sharp end of the tools. This block also enables me to put it in a vice if necessary, so that both my hands are free.

Finally, a thick leather apron is also useful to prevent chisels going into your leg if they slip. It will also protect against slips with power tools to some extent.

Gloves suitable for carving.

Thick leather apron for protection.

Dust and small particles

When using power tools, dust and small wood particles fly everywhere. The larger pieces can accidentally fly into your eyes whilst the smaller particles may go into your lungs. The finer ones often stay in the air and float around for ages. So for prolonged work, use a helmet with a pull-down visor and a fan inside. The fan sucks the air through a filter into the helmet and the positive pressure stops particles from coming under the visor and flying into your eyes. Its battery can be clipped onto a belt around your waist.

It is worth going for a more expensive dust extractor or ideally an air filter, as many of the cheaper versions only pick up the large shavings and leave the finer dust particles floating around in the air. Protect your lungs and eyes; they are irreplaceable! For short spells of machine carving or sanding you can simply use a face mask and goggles - although be aware that goggles can mist up when using a face mask.

Eyesight

Light

If the weather is warm, I like to sit on my garden seat to carve so as to take advantage of the best light available – natural daylight. This makes it much easier to carve fine detail on a netsuke, such as hair or feathers. Back in the workshop, try to carve near a window if possible and ensure that the workshop is well lit. An adjustable lamp is useful for spotlighting a carving. Bandsaws and other machine tools should also be lit. Trying to operate these in the shadows is dangerous.

Magnification

Extra magnification will help you to see the small detail more clearly. There are many different types of magnifier available, from static lenses on a stand to flip-down lenses which clip onto your glasses. Some even have inbuilt lights, but the main thing is not to strain your eyes. Look around to find the one that works best for you. Before buying your own, borrow one to try it out.

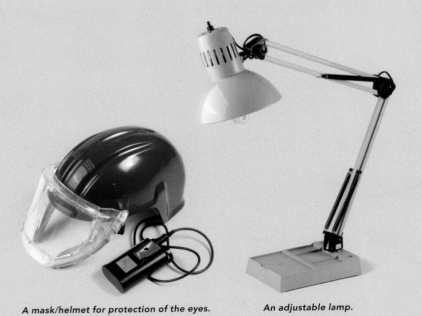

A mask/helmet for protection of the eyes.   **An adjustable lamp.**   **Magnifier with a flip-down lens.**

In the workshop

Clutter

Workshops have all kinds of clutter on the floor which can cause you to trip. It doesn't matter how many shelves you put up, there is always wood and other stuff on the floor. A clear floor gives you freedom of movement and means that you are less likely to trip over. Even loose shoe laces can be a trip hazard, so always tie them securely. This is especially important when you are working with power tools.

Electricity supply

Always switch off all the electricity when leaving the workshop as an electrical fault can easily cause a fire. Get into the habit of checking that all appliances are switched off.

First-aid kit

Keep an up-to-date and well-stocked first-aid kit in your workshop, so that it is easily accessible in the case of a cut or any other injury.

Fire

Some finishing oils can cause a spontaneous fire if they are left to dry on a screwed-up cloth. Always read the instructions on the container and let the cloth dry outside or dispose of it safely to avoid a fire. Also, keep sawdust and wood shavings to a minimum to reduce the risk of fire.

Communication

In case of an emergency in the workshop, it is wise to have some type of communication with which to access help, either a cordless or a mobile phone. The chances are that you will be unlikely to need it, but on that one occasion when you do, it needs be there and ready to use.

Finally...

Keep safety in mind at all times. Think carefully about what you are doing and how best to do it safely.

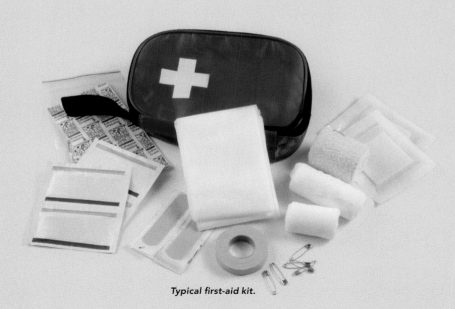

Typical first-aid kit.

TECHNIQUES

EYES

The eyes can enhance or spoil a carving. They appear to bring sight to the netsuke and add expression. However, if they are in the wrong place, or they are not properly aligned, the carving will look wrong. So care is needed to position the eyes in the right place and in relation to each other. Here I show how the technique of adding eyes is carried out and the effect that it has.

Dowel process

First, draw the positions of the eyes in pencil **1**. Check their position several times by looking at the carving from all directions. If in doubt, rub it out. Only start the inlaying process when you are completely satisfied.

With a circular burr cutter held in a multi-tool, drill the eye socket to a depth of around ⁵⁄₃₂in (4mm) **2**. If you do not have a cutter of the right diameter, use a smaller cutter and, after drilling to the right depth, gradually enlarge the hole by moving the cutter around the hole's perimeter right up to the pencil line marking the edge of the eye **3**.

The eye inserts are first made into dowels of around 2 to 2½in (50 to 62mm) in length with the grain running along the dowel **4**. These should be square or rectangular in cross-section and should also be larger than the intended eye size. These dowels can be cut out using a bandsaw or a coping saw. Rotate the dowel on a sanding wheel to ensure that it is shaped as required, with a slight taper towards the end.

In this example an imitation-ivory dowel has been selected **5**. Shape one end, then check the dowel in the eye socket and file it by hand until it is a good tight fit in the eye **6**.

When the dowel fits tightly in the eye socket, remove it, then put some glue into the socket and push it in tight. Cut off the dowel a few millimetres from the socket, using a ⁵⁄₆₄in (2mm) cutter **7**.

1 The eye drawn ready for drilling.

2 The drilled eye needs enlarging.

3 The eye has been enlarged.

4 Imitation ivory, buffalo horn and African blackwood dowels, with the ends shaped and tapered.

5 The toad and its intended imitation-ivory dowel.

6 Dowel inserted to check the fit.

Reshape the dowel for the other eye and repeat the process. When both eyes have been inserted leave them to dry overnight. The following day, shape them with a flat needle file so that they are both uniformly round **8**. Be careful not to mark the head with the file whilst shaping the eyes.

7 Both the dowels have been glued in and cut off.

8 The eyes have been rounded off.

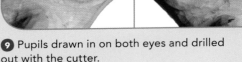

9 Pupils drawn in on both eyes and drilled out with the cutter.

10 Dowel being test-fitted in the eye.

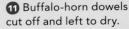

11 Buffalo-horn dowels cut off and left to dry.

12 The eye after polishing with a Micro-Mesh stick.

Next, draw the position of the pupil on each eye before drilling a hole with the ⁵⁄₆₄in (2mm) round cutter in each **9**.

Take a buffalo-horn dowel and roll it on the rotary sanding wheel to make a taper. Test-fit it into one eye **10**.

When the first pupil fits well, remove it from the hole, put glue in the socket and return the dowel. Cut the dowel off a millimetre or so from the eye, then leave to dry **11**.

Reshape the dowel for the other eye and repeat the process. Be careful not to push the dowel in too hard or the imitation ivory might split. If this happens, drill it out and start again.

Once both pupils are dry, shape them with a flat needle file. Using a Micro-Mesh stick, go through the four grades of paper on the stick until the eyes really shine **12**.

When putting in the eyes on various small birds, such as wrens or sparrows, just a simple black eye is sufficient. The colour of the eye can be varied by using different-coloured wood or other materials. I have used many combinations to achieve the effects I require.

13 The eyes have been drilled out.

14 The shaped piece of amber test-fitted into the gilded eye socket.

15 End view of the amber eye drilled to make the pupil.

16 Pupil inked in with a fine-tipped pen.

17 The eye has been glued in and cut off.

18 The eye has been roughly shaped.

19 The finished eye after polishing.

20 Front view showing both eyes in place.

Amber

Making eyes from amber is a different proposition, as it is only available in small pieces which can be difficult to hold. Amber comes in a range of colours ranging from very pale to relatively dark. If you want an eye that is transparent avoid the milky-coloured amber. Here, I am going to show you how to inlay amber eyes into a netsuke owl.

First, drill the eye with a ¼in (6mm) rotary cutter **13**. The bottom of the hole should be concave. Take a piece of amber and round off one end. Test-fit this to ensure that it fits in well, then remove it **14**.

Gild both eye sockets with a gold varnish **15**. Polish the sides of the amber with a Micro-Mesh stick to allow the gilded socket to show through as much as possible.

Drill out the bottom of the amber with a ⁵⁄₆₄in (2mm) cutter to make the pupil **16**. Ink this in with a fine-tipped black pen **17**.

Place some glue just inside the rim of the eye and put the amber in, holding it still for at least 30 seconds. Leave it for a few hours before cutting off the excess with a ⁵⁄₆₄in (2mm) round cutter held in a multi-tool **18**. Use the same tool to gently shape the eye into a small dome, before using a flat needle file to refine the shape **19**.

Go all over the eye with the four grades on a Micro-Mesh stick, to create a transparent eye with a pupil and the gold socket showing through **20**. The domed eye will act like a magnifying glass and makes the pupil look larger than it actually is. If the amber is long enough it is a good idea to make the other eye with the same piece of amber, so that the colour remains consistent.

21 The design has been drawn on and hollowed out.

22 The eye socket is carved out and drawn onto the paua shell.

23 Partly shaped paua eye with most of the shell cut away.

24 The completed paua-shell insert.

25 The hole drilled for the pupil.

26 Buffalo-horn pupil inserted.

Shell

Eyes made from shell, such as mother of pearl or paua shell, are very thin so they have to be inlaid like a veneer. This means making a shallow recess in the surface close to the thickness of the shell and shaping the recess to the required shape of the eye. The shell is then cut and filed until it fits the recess.

For this example, I have used a manju netsuke with a dragon design and paua shell for the eyes. The first step is to draw the design onto a piece of boxwood **21**. Next, cut the oval for the eye, by pressing a ⁵⁄₃₂in (4mm) No.9 gouge into the sides of the eye and a ³⁄₃₂in (2.5mm) No.7 gouge into the top and bottom of the eye to outline it. With a ¹⁄₁₆in (1.5mm) No.1 chisel, clear out the area inside the oval of the eye down to the thickness of the shell you are using.

Draw the shape of the eye in black ink on the paua shell, so that it is easy to see **22**. Use a ³⁄₆₄in (1mm) tapered cutter held in a multi-tool to cut it out **23**. After separation from the main shell, you may well find that the piece of paua is difficult to hold in your hands for the final shaping with the needle file. Usually I file it with a small box on my lap so I can catch it if it drops.

Put glue into the hole, insert the eye and leave it to dry **24**. Once it has dried, drill a hole for the pupil and insert a buffalo-horn dowel **25** **26**. File the dowel to complete the eye.

BUMPS

Bumps, large or small, cover the skin of a number of creatures. Carving them can be a laborious process, but your hard work will pay off and will make the finished carving into something special.

Carving bumps

There are three ways to carve bumps. The first is to carve them all with a small gouge, the second is to use a multi-tool with a small round cutter, and the third is a unique Japanese method called *ukibori* which produces very small bumps.

I shall demonstrate the three different methods on the same toad. To do this I will carve the various bumps on separate parts of the toad so that you can see the difference clearly.

Gouge

Start by drawing the bumps on the surface, leaving room between them to carve the background down by about $\frac{1}{32}$in (0.5mm) **1**. Use a $\frac{1}{16}$in (1.5mm) gouge to carve around the bumps and to clear out the areas between them **2**. This will leave the background a little ragged, so use a small circular needle file or a flat needle file to effectively round off the tops of the bumps **3**. It is not essential for the background to be perfectly smooth.

1 Bumps drawn on the toad's back.

2 Bumps carved and spaces between them cleared out.

3 Background cleaned up and tops of bumps rounded off.

4 Bumps drawn onto the toad's back

5 Bumps carved and spaces cleared with a circular cutter.

6 Background cleaned up and top of bumps rounded off.

7 Bumps pressed into the surface.

8 The wood has now been carved down to the bottom of the dents.

Rotary cutter

This method is very similar to carving around the bumps by hand, as the small round cutter does the same job as the gouge. The difference between the two methods is negligible, although making the bumps with the rotary cutter is much quicker and easier to control.

Draw the bumps onto the netsuke and cut round the outside with a ³⁄₆₄in (1mm) circular cutter held in your multi-tool **4** **5**. The cutter can be up to about ⁵⁄₆₄in (2mm) diameter and still do the job well. With care it is possible to round off the edges of the bumps with the same cutter and file or sand them down to make them round or oval **6**. Ensure that you have also cleaned up the background.

Ukibori method

This is a traditional Japanese method often used to create a number of small bumps all together. To demonstrate the process, I worked on the area between the eyes, forward towards the toad's mouth and under the chin.

The tool for making *ukibori* bumps has a small round end to it (see page 24). Make sure that the surface of the netsuke is smooth before starting. Push the rounded end of the tool into the surface of the netsuke to make a number of depressions where the bumps are required **7**.

Carve the wood right down to the bottom of the depressions **8**. Then, paint hot water across the whole area with a clean brush. The depressed areas will rise up above the surrounding surface.

9 After wetting with hot water, the bumps have swollen back up above the surface.

10 The completed *ukibori* bumps.

11 The square- and round-section bradawls.

12 Sparrow pecking completed on one side with square-shaft bradawl.

Once the netsuke has dried, the small bumps will remain across the surface as the hot water makes the compressed wood swell back up to its original height **9**. The bumps are small, so they can easily be sanded away; therefore only use Micro-Mesh to lightly buff the netsuke **10**.

Sparrow pecking

This is a centuries-old technique used to make the foreground stand out and the background appear to recede. For larger carvings, it involves banging a bradawl, or a pointed nail, all over the background, with the tool held between your forefinger and thumb while your little finger rests on the surface and acts like a spring.

The 'up and down' movement resembles a sparrow pecking, hence the name. When you have mastered this technique, a large area can be covered quickly.

For the netsuke, push a bradawl with a square or circular cross-section into the wood all round the bumps carved on the surface **11**. This will make the bumps appear as if they have increased in height. Circular or square cross-section bradawls produce very slight differences in effect.

Afterwards, brush the surface with a darker wax which will lie in the small holes and remain there after polishing. The wax will increase the contrast between the bumps and the background **12**. (The sparrow pecking effect can also be made with power tools, see page 28).

HAIR

Carving the many different types of hair takes both time and patience to master. With practice you can make shallow or deep, short or long cuts, using a fine V-tool. Be aware that the hardness of the wood will affect the results.

Long hair

Draw the hair in pencil on a small area of the carving. It is not possible to carve the entire length of a piece of hair in one cut. So, cut part of the way with a 1/16in (1.5mm) V-tool, lift it out of the cut, then put it back into the same cut and extend it a little further. In this way you can make both long and curved cuts. So that the hair does not appear too flat, carve some of the areas down below the adjacent hair, re-cutting some of the lines as necessary ❶.

Short hair

Carving short hair simply requires a short cut with a 1/16in (1.5mm) V-tool. It takes practice to control the length of the cuts and to ensure that they are the same length, so practice on a spare piece of wood beforehand ❷.

To create short, curly hair, change the direction of the cut within a short distance. Start by drawing the curly hair lines, and making a short curving cut along the pencil line with the V-tool. Take the tool out of the cut, then replace it and change direction to follow the next part of the curve. Keep repeating this process until the stroke is complete. In time you will be able to complete the cut in one go ❸.

❶ Billy goat, showing long and curved hair.

❷ Lots of short cuts will make the surface look like short hair.

❸ Curly hair used on a camel netsuke.

SCALES

Scales on animals, such as fish or snakes, can be carved in three separate ways. There are noticeable differences between these three methods, which I will demonstrate here.

Gouge

The first method uses a small gouge, the same size and shape as the scales. This is pressed straight into the surface of the netsuke to mark the outline of each scale. To increase the visual effect, a small fillet can be removed from behind each scale with an angled chisel. This produces well-defined scales **1**.

V-tool

The second method is to cut the shape of the scales with a V-tool **2**. Afterwards, the fillet can be removed from behind the scales with an angled chisel. This is the hardest method as it means carving very tight curves.

Impression

Finally, you can choose not to carve individual scales, but instead to use a V-tool to carve curved lines across the body at an angle to each other to give the overall impression of scales. This method was used on the gobi fish shown below **3**. It is a very useful technique to master as the scales of many fish and snakes are incredibly small.

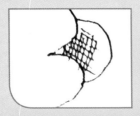

The shaded area is the fillet which is removed.

1 Scales on a carp carved with a gouge.

2 Scales on the snake carved with a V-tool.

3 Scales on a gobi fish using the impression method.

FEATHERS

Feathers on a bird are carved in a similar way to the first two methods described for carving scales, although a little more detail needs to be added so as to make them appear as lifelike feathers, rather than scales.

In practice

The feathers on the first owl were carved with a small gouge. A ¹⁄₁₆in (1.5mm) V-tool was also used to put in the barb lines on the edges of the feathers and the central shaft **1**. The feathers on the second owl were shaped using a ¹⁄₁₆in

(1.5mm) V-tool with only two almost parallel cuts to indicate the shaft on each feather **2**. The final owl shows how only the central shaft has been carved on the feathers **3**.

1 Feathered edging used.

2 A more simplified feather with just the central shaft carved.

3 The final completed netsuke owl.

Various examples of carved feathers on different birds.

SHELLS

Snail shells and their bodies require a lot of texturing in order to make them look realistic, but they are well worth the investment in time it takes to learn the skill. The process between the body and the shell is very different, as you will see.

Texturing

To texture the surface of a snail's shell, make a long cut with a V-tool across a roundish surface. The difficulty of carving such cuts is influenced by the hardness of the wood. If it is very soft the cuts can break out at the sides, yet if it is too hard the cuts can skid off the surface. Boxwood, pear, holly, and apple wood are all good for carving shells.

In practice

First, draw the hair lines onto the surface of the shell ❶. Using a ¹⁄₁₆in (1.5mm) V-tool, make a short cut along the line, before removing the tool ❷. Rotate the shell, put the V-tool back in the cut and extend it.

Repeat the process until the whole length of the cut is completed. Now, the trick is to carve another long cut, alongside and very close to the first, but preventing the new cut from running into the previous one. If this does happen, simply start another cut further along the same line and work back to where the two lines cut into each other ❸. Once you have carved the whole shell's surface, you are unlikely to notice a few little mistakes.

Where it is not possible to make cuts with the V-tool, such as in between the horns, press a ¹⁄₁₆in (1.5mm) flat chisel into the surface and follow the V-tool lines on each side ❹.

❶ Pencil lines drawn near the mouth of the shell.

❷ The first few lines carved in.

❸ The carving as it progresses.

❹ Carving between the horns.

5 The long lines drawn on the body.

6 The long lines cut with a V-tool.

7 The short cuts made perpendicular to the long ones.

8 A sketch of the long and short cuts used.

9 The various cuts used to represent the snail's body surface.

Pink ivory snail.

Tagua-nut snail.

Carving the body of a snail to represent its bumpy surface can be achieved by long cuts along the body and short cuts across the long cuts. All the lines are drawn to follow any curves or twists on the body **5**.

Make all the long cuts first with a ¹⁄₁₆in (1.5mm) V-tool **6**. Do not include the head or the skirt of the body at this stage.

Next, create all the very short cuts perpendicular to the long ones with the V-tool **7**. The short cuts go across and between the two long cuts **8** **9**.

When making the cross cuts there is a tendency for bits to come out, especially if the grain is too open, so it is advisable to use a close-grained wood like boxwood or holly.

INLAYING

A wide range of materials can be used to inlay eyes and also to enhance other areas of netsuke carvings. I have carved five netsuke which have been inlaid in places other than the eyes. I will explain how to carve these pieces to show you how to inlay your own carvings with various materials.

Blue dragon

The first netsuke I inlaid in this way was this New Zealand blue dragon for which I used paua shell, a thin blue-green shell which captures the light.

When the surface of the netsuke has been curved, as here, follow the shape with the shell by cutting it into platelets, which interlock with each other.

First, cut a recess in the body to accept the shell, then cut the shell with a fine cutter held firmly in a multi-tool. Fit each piece into the recess with the platelet next to it, and glue it in so that the inlay progresses along the recess from one end to the other. If you prefer you can use wood veneers or mother of pearl to produce a different effect.

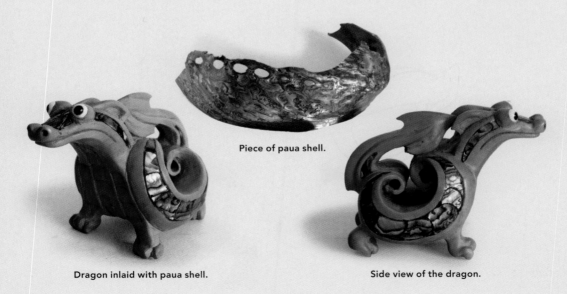

Piece of paua shell.

Dragon inlaid with paua shell.

Side view of the dragon.

Badger cubs

The second netsuke I inlaid was of two fighting badger cubs. African blackwood was inlaid into the lime body to create the black and white faces. First draw on the outline of the faces. As the faces are curved, make a relatively deep recess in which to insert the blackwood. Keep offering the wood up to each recess, shaving a bit off, then trying again until it fits in well. Glue in each piece one by one. They will be shaped afterwards to follow the contours of each face and to leave the ears sticking up.

Next, drill through the blackwood for the white patches around the eyes. Insert the white lime dowels as shown in the process for making eyes (see pages 42–3). Into these insert buffalo-horn eye dowels as these shine up well when polished. To create the white patches on the ears, drill the shapes to the required size and again insert lime dowels cut to fit the shape of the recesses. To complete the face, glue a piece of buffalo horn on for the nose; this will shine well and resemble a wet nose.

Fighting badger cubs inlaid with African blackwood.

The badger cubs viewed from the side.

Tortoise

The tortoise was completed by inlaying the boxwood shell with laburnum dowels, shaped like the segments of the shell. Shape each recess to the corresponding segment of the shell, and tailor-make the dowels to fit each recess. This is fundamentally the same process as inlaying eyes (see page 42–3).

Tortoise inlaid to show separate segments of the shell.

1 Part-finished blue-ringed octopus.

2 Blue resin, showing the black layer.

3 Resin turned onto its side to show the shape to be inserted.

4 Hole drilled for insert.

5 Insert glued in place.

6 Insert shaped and polished.

Completed blue ringed octopus.

Octopus

The fourth netsuke to be inlaid was a blue-ringed octopus carved in boxwood. Here, I have shown it partly finished to begin with to show how the process develops **1**. Using a blue resin stick with a black layer just below the surface, make a slightly domed dowel to produce a blue and black ring effect **2**.

The main difficulty here is in inlaying the dowel. It cannot be inlaid in the conventional way as the black layer runs along the dowel. So, it is best to make small round inlay inserts across the main direction of the grain as shown **3**. Once you have drilled a hole for the insert **4**, shape the resin stick to the required size. Cut it off the resin stick and glue it into place before shaping and polishing the insert **5** **6**.

Mandarin duck

The fifth and final netsuke which I have made using inlay is the mandarin duck shown on pages 100–9. I will not repeat it here, except to show a photograph of the finished netsuke where the inlay can be clearly seen.

Inlaid mandarin duck.

Carving Other Materials

Most of my netsuke are carved in wood as it is easier to carve and often much more colourful than other materials. However, there are various additional materials from which to carve netsuke, especially ivory and tagua nut (vegetable ivory).

Carving ivory

So far I have only carved three ivory netsuke, so my experience is very limited. In all three cases, I used modern techniques rather than those used by the early netsuke carvers. The basic removal of material is done with cutters in a multi-tool, as this takes you close to the finished shape of each netsuke. Smooth the surface by filing, scraping, then sanding.

Carve the features, such as the stripes and hair on this tiger, with a small V-tool **1**. If you find that these cuts are too wide, try using a steel stylus. The tiger was my first ever ivory carving and about my fifth ever netsuke carving, so I was still in the rapid-learning process. I would carve the stripes and hair much more finely if I repeated it.

Carving tagua nut

Tagua nut is hard, yet it can be carved with carving tools or with cutters held in a multi-tool. These roundish nuts, which vary in size between 1–2in (25–50mm) in length, are usually purchased with a brown skin covering the nut itself **2**.

1 A traditional Japanese tiger in ivory.

2 A basic tagua nut with its skin still on.

3 The skin cleaned off to reveal the hole.

4 The outline drawn on one side.

5 Rough outline after cutting out the profile.

6 A little more general shaping of the body.

A working sketch of the pelican.

This skin can be scraped off or removed with a cutter, which is much quicker. This will reveal a small hole at one end which occurs in all nuts and is part of their growing process **3**. This hole needs to be considered when selecting your netsuke subject and your design so that it does not interfere with the overall shape.

In practice

Here I have carved a simple pelican netsuke in tagua nut to show the various stages in its development. First, draw a sketch of the subject with pencil or fine black pen **4**. You may well find that the marks rub off, so only draw on the bit that you are working on. Hold the nut in a carpenter's vice and cut the side elevation shape in stages with a coping saw. Start rough-shaping the pelican with ¼in (6mm) and ⅛in (3mm) cutters **5**. Continue shaping the body of the pelican until you are satisfied with the shape **6**.

7 The bottom of the pouch defined.

8 The bottom of the pouch is undercut and the lower mandible is cut in.

9 The lower mandible cut in a bit deeper and the join cut in lightly.

10 Beak lines sharpened, pouch shaped, and the two lines on top of the upper mandible cut in.

11 The side view of the pelican with a pouch full of fish.

12 Eyes, beak and eye surround drawn on.

Roughly draw on the line where the lower mandible joins the pouch and define the bottom of the pouch **7**. Undercut the bottom of the pouch with a ⅛in (3mm) cutter, then lightly cut in the lower edge of the bottom mandible **8**.

Next, cut in the lower mandible slightly deeper, and lightly cut in the join between the upper and lower beak mandible using a ⅛in (3mm) cutter **9**.

Shape the pouch and sharpen the beak lines with a 1/16in (1.5mm) V-tool, cutting in the two lines of the upper mandible with the same tool **10**. The pelican now appears full of character with a pouch brimming with a full catch **11**.

Now, draw on the positions of the eyes, the bald area that surrounds them, the edge of the beak and the pouch where it meets the head **12**.

13 Buffalo-horn eyes let in and polished.

14 Outline of tail and wing feathers drawn.

15 Tail and rear of wings shaped.

16 Tuft at the back of the head just showing.

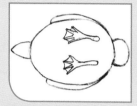

17 Sketch of the feet on the underside.

18 The feet carved.

19 The carving process close to finishing.

With a ³⁄₆₄in (1mm) drill, make the eye sockets before shaping a buffalo-horn dowel to insert into the eyes (see pages 42–3). File the eyes down until they are round, then polish them with a Micro-Mesh stick **13**.

The next stage is to draw the ends of the large wings and the tail on the tagua nut **14**. Shape these using a ¹⁄₈in (3mm) cutter, before carving a small tuft at the back of the head **15** **16**. When carving, even with the sharpest chisels and gouges, the chips removed are very thin and very small, but do not be discouraged, because slowly and surely the shape will develop.

Sketch the feet on the underside of the carving and carve them using a ¹⁄₈in (3mm) square-ended cutter for the outside shape. I cut away the areas between the feet with a ¹⁄₁₆in (1.5mm) No.1 chisel and marked in the details for the toes with a ¹⁄₁₆in (1.5mm) V-tool **17** **18**. The feet will become clearer when they have been inked in (see pages 62–3). The carving process on the pelican is now almost complete: all that is left to do is to sand and polish the piece, and add the holes for the cord **19** (see page 69). The feather details will become clearer when they are inked in.

COLOUR

Many netsuke carvings have been enhanced by adding colour to some of the carved features on the surface, such as hair on the surface of ivory. In some cases one or more colours were applied to make the netsuke appear more realistic.

Ink

Inking in the features on an ivory or tagua-nut netsuke ensures that they stand out clearly as they contrast with the white background. It also makes the whole piece more appealing and lifelike. I have used this technique to emphasize the bumps of a toad, the fur of a tiger and the hair of a charging wild boar. The inks can be bought in a wide variety of colours from all good art shops and can be used straight away without any preparation.

The process is simple, run Indian ink into the recesses with an old-fashioned dip-in nib. When the ink is dry, scrape or finely sand the piece to leave a clean finish with the ink confined inside the carved recesses. Alternatively you can use a fine-line pen, with water- and fade-proof pigment ink and a fine-tipped point, to ink in each carved recess. Go over it all again with the pen before cleaning and polishing it to check if there are any areas which need improving. I used this method successfully to ink in the features on a tagua-nut pelican **1**.

Dye

Fabric dye is available in a considerable range of colours. I prefer to use Dylon fabric dye which comes in powder form in small non-resealable containers **2**. The numbers on the tins indicate the colour of the dye from the Dylon colour chart. Since only a very small amount is used for each netsuke, it is useful to have some small containers to put the excess powder in for future use.

The main purpose of dyeing a netsuke is to colour the surface of the piece to ensure that the details show up. Dye the whole netsuke with a coloured dye, then sand off the high spots to give a slight colour contrast between the high bits and the background. The netsuke dormouse, for example, has been dyed to show darker colour in the carved recesses **3**.

Another good reason to use dye is to bring out a particular feature and to make it look more realistic. An example is the black and white colouring on a netsuke panda, without which it wouldn't resemble the real thing at all.

1 Ink being applied, and the inked-in features on the pelican netsuke.

2 Fabric dye comes in many colours.

3 Netsuke dyed to show darker colour in the carved recesses.

The process of dyeing a netsuke is relatively straightforward. Place a little amount of powder of the selected colour into a suitable container, add a little warm water and stir. Test the colour on a piece of the same wood and add more dye until you get the colour you require **4**.

Prepare the piece by painting it with warm water. Allow this to soak in for at least ten minutes before painting on the dye with a clean brush. Leave the carving to dry, then judge whether a second coat of dye is necessary. Sand or scrape the high spots to get the contrast you require.

In practice

Here, I have used a toad to show you the process stage-by-stage. The bumps on the toad have been finished all over **5**. I have also separated the toad from its block, but have kept this piece to test the dye colour before applying it to the actual carving.

4 Powder has been added to water to test the colour.

5 The finished toad is ready for dyeing.

6 The toad is wetted with clean water and left to dry before the dye is applied.

7 The first coat of dye is now dry and I decided to add another coat.

8 The second coat of dye is also dry and the high spots have been sanded off.

9 Masking fluid being applied.

10 The finished snail ready for colouring.

11 Real-life model.

12 The masking fluid painted onto the body.

13 With coffee-coloured dye added.

Wet the netsuke with clean water and leave it to sink in **6**. Then apply the first coat of dye to the netsuke. When it is dry, judge whether you need to add a second coat **7**. Leave this to dry, before sanding off the high spots with a Micro-Mesh stick **8**. The colour contrast between the high spots and low spots should now be obvious.

Masking off areas

If you decide to dye selected parts of a netsuke, ensure that the surface of the wood is dry, then use watercolour painter's masking fluid to coat the areas that are going to remain natural **9**. Add dye or wax to the rest of the piece. I will demonstrate this by applying masking fluid to the body of a carved snail whilst I dye the shell, then colour the body using a soft coloured wax **10**.

I found a snail in the garden and brought him indoors to pose for this photograph **11**. He was too shy to show his face, but his shell is quite colourful and very useful for getting a good idea of the general colouring.

Apply masking fluid to the body of the snail at the intersection with the shell **12**. It is only necessary to paint on enough fluid so that when the shell is dyed it will not run onto the body. Next, mix coffee-coloured dye with water as shown earlier. This time make the colour slightly darker by adding more powder. Paint the dye on all over the shell and leave to dry **13**.

Apply the second coat more randomly to make it appear speckled **14**. When this has dried, sand off some of the high spots to provide more

14 The second coat of dye added and the high spots sanded.

15 The darker patches on the shell inked in.

16 Masking layer removed.

17 Antique Pine wax being applied.

18 The wax brushed onto the body.

19 The polished netsuke.

20 Hard wax sticks.

contrast to the shell. Using a fine-tipped black ink pen, draw some of the dark markings onto the shell **15**. Wait until it is dry, then peel off the masking layer to reveal the body underneath **16**.

Wax

Soft wax

Colouring the body with soft wax is the next stage; it is also another way of colouring a netsuke. Liberon make a number of different-coloured soft waxes which can be brushed on and polished off, leaving the high spots lighter than the low spots. Where you have sparrow-pecked backgrounds, such as around the bumps on a toad, the wax will lie in the indentations, making them darker and adding emphasis.

For the snail, I shall use Liberon's Antique Pine wax. This looks very dark when it is first applied, but when it is polished off it only makes the

colour of the wood slightly darker **17**. Brush the wax into all the recesses on the body and leave it to soak in for about 30 minutes **18**.

Then polish it off with a soft cloth **19**. When the wax has been polished off, the slightly darker wax remains in the low spots.

Hard wax

Hard wax inlay is another way of colouring parts of a netsuke. In this case the wax comes in sticks which are rubbed into narrow V or U cuts **20**. The heat generated by rubbing the sticks onto the wood melts the wax sufficiently for it to fill the grooves. When the rubbing stops the wax simply goes hard again.

21 Black wax rubbed into the grooves of the cuttlefish.

22 Grey wax has been rubbed into the carved hair on these cubs.

23 The Trianon gold has been used on the top two fish and the Versailles gold on the lower one.

24 Gilding varnish being applied.

25 The two bottles of bleach chemicals.

The surplus can then be sanded or scraped off so that the wax is level with the surface of the wood and contrasts with the main colour of the wood. I have used this method to make the dark markings on a cuttlefish body and to make the fur grey on a pair of fighting badger cubs to imitate their real colour **21**, **22**.

Paint

Painting a netsuke is slightly different from the process of dyeing it. The latter is transparent and leaves the wood grain visible, whereas painting completely obscures the wood grain. Many Japanese netsuke were painted to show particular elements, for example, the dress on a dancer, or robes on a warrior, etc. Acrylic paints are the most suitable for painting a netsuke.

Gilding

To create small areas of gold, I prefer to use a gilding varnish which can be painted on, rather than gold leaf which can be difficult to apply particularly in small, confined spaces. Gold varnish comes in many different shades. In the picture above the two fish at the top have been gilded with Trianon coloured Liberon gilt varnish, while the bottom fish has been gilded with the Versailles gold gilt **23**, **24**. This gives you some idea of the colours available.

Bleach

To bleach carvings I prefer to use a two-part system, such as Rustins bleach **25**. This wood bleach comes in two bottles, marked A and B, and will only work on bare wood. If used correctly the wood will go a much lighter colour.

Apply solution A to clean, dry wood with a brush and leave for 10–20 minutes before applying the other solution. Do the same with the B solution but leave it for a minimum of 3–4 hours. The process can be repeated with both solutions after two hours if the wood is very dark or if it is badly stained. A crust may form on the surface which should be wiped off with a damp rag or a scrubbing brush. The wood should then be washed in a mixture of 1 pint (0.6 litre) of water and 1tsp of white vinegar. Then leave it to dry.

FINAL STEPS

We are almost there, yet the finishing and polishing can make a big difference to the end result. Spend as much time as you need repeatedly going over the netsuke, cleaning it up and sanding it before polishing it.

Finishing

Finishing the netsuke means going all over it, including underneath, looking for small things to improve or tidy, such as rounding off bumps which are too angular, or giving better definition to the outline of a feather and so on. If the dye is obscuring something that should be seen, simply scrape it off. When all these little things have been done, go over all the carving with a Micro-Mesh sanding stick. For the most part you will only need to use the finest two grades to create a smooth shine all over.

1 Here my name has been burnt in with a pyrography pen on this boxwood octopus.

2 I have carved my name on the underside of this ivory toad in an oval reserve before inking it in.

Signing your work

I recommend that you always add your signature to your work. You have spent a lot of valuable time designing, planning and making a unique carving and you should take the credit for it. People buying my work always expect to see my signature on the piece. I am lucky in having a short surname which does not take up much space. If you have a longer name then at least put your initials on, or something that clearly identifies you as the maker.

You can sign your name in at least three ways. A pyrography pen burns your name into the surface **1**. However, sometimes this burns better in one area than another due to the grain of the wood, causing the signature letters to vary in size. Where you cannot burn your name, such as on buffalo horn or ivory, carve your name on the piece instead **2**.

3 My signature in a rectangular reserve signed with an ink pen.

4 Here are the three clear waxes that I use the most.

The third option is to use an ink pen and to hope that the ink remains permanent **3**.

Japanese netsuke carvers often sign their names in a little cartouche or reserve as this adds to the special nature of the signature. This reserve is usually rectangular or oval.

If you think signing your name in a reserve or cartouche would spoil the netsuke, you can always sign it without a surround or choose somewhere convenient that does not spoil the overall effect of the carving.

If you find that there is space you can also add the date. This means that people can tell when it was carved. One of the problems with old netsuke is knowing how old they are, as many of them were not dated.

Polishing

The very last step in the process is to polish the netsuke. I usually use a clear wax polish, such as Liberon clear fine paste wax, Renaissance wax or neutral shoe polish **4**.

Renaissance polish is made from refined waxes blended into a formula used by the British Museum and international restoration specialists to revive and protect valuable furniture, leather, paintings, metals, marble and ivory. It freshens colours and imparts a soft sheen.

Apply the clear wax with a small brush, and leave it on for about 15 minutes. Then polish the netsuke, first with a clean brush to remove any wax from the low spots, then with a cloth. Keep polishing until you have achieved a nice sheen. Your carving may benefit from repeating this process a week or so later.

CORD HOLES

Netsuke would traditionally have two holes (*himotoshi*) in them, so that the cord could be passed through them. Some pieces have a natural opening, others require the holes to be drilled into them. The two holes are located close to each other and are connected together below the surface so that the cord can pass through both of them.

Choose the location of the holes carefully so as not to spoil the look of the carving. Try to find a place where they will appear fairly unobtrusive, usually on the underside.

In practice

With a circular-ended cutter held in a multi-tool, drill two identical holes vertically into the netsuke at a depth of around ¼–⁵⁄₁₆in (6–8mm) with a diameter of ⅛–⁵⁄₃₂in (3–4mm). Ensure that you leave a space of about ⁵⁄₁₆in (8mm) between the centres. If you increase the diameter of the

holes to take a thicker cord, you also need to increase the depth of the holes and the spacing between them.

With the drill running, carefully put the cutter in one hole. When the cutter is completely below the surface, move the shaft outwards and the cutter inwards towards the other hole. Repeat the process for the second hole. The drill should run into the recess from the first hole. Practice this process on a spare piece of wood as many times as necessary until you feel confident.

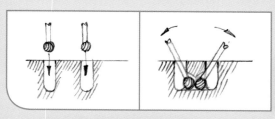

A sketch showing how the two holes are drilled and then connected.

The cord holes drilled into an octopus and a nautilus netsuke.

THE CARVING PROCESS

Getting Started

The overriding philosophy of netsuke carving is that the time it takes is irrelevant; the objective is to make the carving as good as you can. This requires lots of patience. If you become frustrated with a particular problem, simply put the carving down and leave it for a while, days if necessary. I always work on several carvings at the same time, so if I have a problem with one I can put it down and start work on another piece while I think about how to solve the issue.

Netsuke were originally designed to be worn with clothes and consequently would have been handled regularly, brushed against clothing and pushed up underneath the belt. Therefore, any protruding bits would have easily broken off, especially on a wooden netsuke where the grain was in the wrong direction. Netsuke should be compact and feel good when held, with no sharp bits or protrusions sticking out. Many modern netsuke designers have forgotten this and whilst the designs and craftsmanship are superb, they would be impractical to wear and use. When you carve your own netsuke pieces, think carefully about which direction the grain is going and use its strength to good effect.

Selecting material

Throughout this book I have chosen to focus on wood as it is the easiest material to obtain and to carve into netsuke; it is therefore ideal for beginners.

To explain the process itself, I selected three types of wood with very different characteristics; lime is easy to carve and readily available; boxwood is hard, but takes very good detail as it is slow-growing and close-grained; and cherry is fairly easy to carve and to obtain, with slightly more colour. When you have carved a few netsuke in wood, you can always move on to other materials which are more challenging.

Holding the wood

The first challenge is how to hold the wood while you carve it. With netsuke being so small and having to be carved all over, including the underside, you have to be able to turn it over in any direction. I eventually developed the art of cutting out two netsuke back to back, so that I could hold the wood by one end and carve the other, then turn it around to hold the finished netsuke while I carved the other end. I carve all my netsuke held in my hand, but you may prefer to put your work in a vice. To do this, leave a square block on one end that can be held in the vice. You can, of course, carve a different netsuke each side of the block as shown below.

Piece of boxwood with an owl on one end and an octopus on the other.

Part-carved blue-ringed octopus in boxwood.

Selection process

Your next step is to decide what you would like to carve. Hopefully the examples shown in this book will help you to select your subject, although I would advise keeping to a simple design for your first one. Select the type of wood that will suit the subject, bearing in mind colour and workability – the ability to achieve the shape and surface texture required. Some species of wood are better suited to a smooth finish, while others are better for detailed carvings.

In the following examples, I will carve two netsuke in each of the three types of wood, in order to take you through the carving process.

For the limewood I have selected a crane and a sleeping wild boar, both of which are traditional Japanese netsuke designs. Using the boxwood I will carve a leveret (a young hare) and a diving frog. In the cherry I will carve a mandarin duck and a bat. In this exercise the grain runs from end to end, i.e. along the wood, on all three blocks.

Sketching

Start by drawing onto paper the side view of each netsuke in detail and to scale.

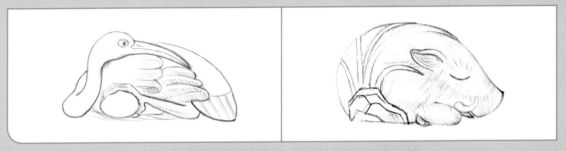

Limewood block for netsuke crane and sleeping wild boar.

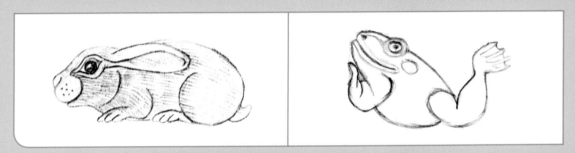

Boxwood block for netsuke leveret and diving frog.

Cherry block for netsuke mandarin duck and bat.

Photocopy the drawings, then transfer them onto the wood by placing a piece of carbon paper on the block of wood, positioning the drawing on top, then drawing round the outside of the netsuke with a pencil – ensure that the paper does not move in the process. When the carbon paper is removed you will see the outline of the netsuke on the wood. Draw over the outline in pencil or fine black ink so that it is easier to see the outline when you are cutting it out. Alternatively, you can glue the photocopy directly onto the wood and cut around the outlines.

The pictures below show the netsuke drawn onto the wood, ready for cutting out.

The next series of photographs shows the three blocks cut out in side profile.

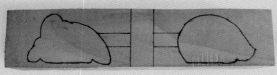

Netsuke crane and sleeping wild boar drawn on lime.

Netsuke crane and sleeping wild boar outlines cut out.

Netsuke leveret and diving frog drawn on boxwood.

Netsuke leveret and diving frog outlines cut out.

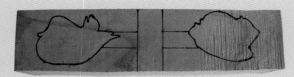

Netsuke mandarin duck and bat drawn on cherry.

Netsuke mandarin duck and bat outlines cut out.

Cutting out

The next step is to cut round the drawings. Use a bandsaw, fret saw or coping saw to achieve the side profile shape, leaving some wood connected to the central block as shown. If any of the shapes are too complicated, just cut wide of the drawing so that the shape can be carved later. It is always better to cut a little outside the line than to cut inside the line.

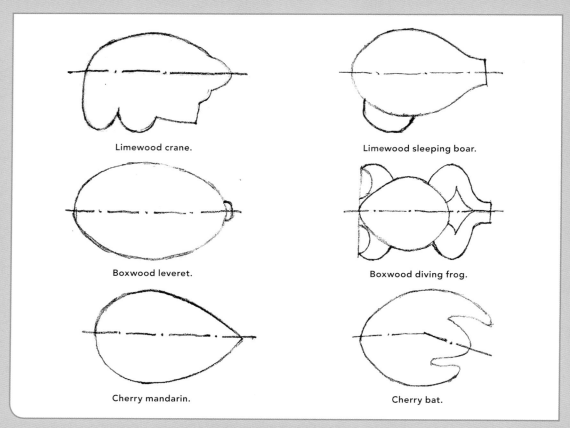

Limewood crane.

Limewood sleeping boar.

Boxwood leveret.

Boxwood diving frog.

Cherry mandarin.

Cherry bat.

Plan views for all six netsuke.

Top view

Draw out the plan views of the netsuke, so you can see what the carvings look like from above. I have drawn these out on paper for the six netsuke involved in this carving exercise, see above.

Transfer the drawings to the partly cut-out blocks so they can be cut out in plan view. Due to the uneven surfaces it is not possible to transfer these onto the wood using carbon paper, as we did for the side views; instead draw them in freehand using pencil. Alternatively, reattach the pieces that have been sawn off to provide a flat surface, holding them together with masking tape.

For each netsuke put in a centre line on the wood. (Note that the head of the bat turns to one side, so there are two centre lines for the body and the head.) As you continue to draw the outlines keep checking the overall width. When you are happy with the outline, ink it in or draw over it in pencil to ensure that it is clear.

The photographs opposite show the netsuke marked out in plan view and ready for cutting. Apart from the frog, they have all been drawn on the upper surface. The outline of the frog was difficult to see, so I turned it over and redrew the outline on the underside to ensure it was clear.

Limewood block with plan view of crane
and sleeping boar drawn on.

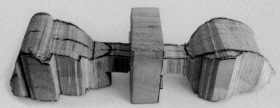

Limewood block now cut out in two
dimensions: side view and plan.

Boxwood block with leveret and diving
frog drawn on the underside.

Boxwood block ready for the
carving process to commence.

Cherry block with mandarin duck and
bat drawn in plan view.

Cherry block showing the mandarin duck and
bat, looking a little unclear at this stage.

Cutting out

Cut the outlines out using a bandsaw, again
cutting wide of the line if necessary. Be careful
as you are working close to the cutting edge,
whilst holding a miniature carving. Always keep
your hands behind or to the side of the cutting
edge and pull the wood from behind the blade
rather than pushing from the front.

Shaping the end view

You can see from the following photographs that
the carvings still do not look like the subjects they
are supposed to represent; that is because we still
have to carve the end view of each piece of wood.
This is where the tricky part starts. Round off each
netsuke carefully, incorporating the main features
whilst improving their overall shape.

Individual pieces

From here on, I will explain the carving process
for each netsuke individually up to the finished
article. Specific carving and finishing techniques
covering such things as inlaying eyes, carving
bumps and surface texturing have already been
covered in the Techniques section.

CRANE

This is the much-loved national bird of Japan. The crane appears in much of the traditional artwork, in paintings, on porcelain, on *inros* and, of course, netsuke. In netsuke carvings mother cranes are often pictured sitting on an egg and sometimes, as this one, holding on to their precious egg.

Materials:

- Limewood block for two netsuke 6 x 1³⁄₈ x 1³⁄₈in (150 x 35 x 35mm)
- Imitation ivory, holly, tagua nut or real ivory to make dowels for the eyes
- Buffalo horn, ebony or African blackwood for the eye pupils

Tools:

Gouges and chisels:

- ³⁄₁₆in (5mm) No.5 gouge
- ¹⁄₄in (6mm) No.7 gouge
- ⁵⁄₃₂in (4mm) No.9 gouge
- ¹⁄₈in (3mm) No.10 gouge
- ¹⁄₁₆in (1.5mm) V-tool
- ¹⁄₁₆in (1.5mm) flat chisel

Cutters:

- ³⁄₆₄in (1mm) and ¹⁄₃₂in (0.5mm) circular cutters for a multi-tool

Files:

- Medium-coarse file
- Needle files

Miscellaneous

Abrasives:

- Sandpaper grits from about 100 to 400
- Micro-Mesh paper, 1800 to 12000 grit
- Micro-Mesh stick with 4 grits on the same stick

Glue:

- Wood glue

Finishes:

- Rustins two-part bleach (optional)
- Clear polish such as clear shoe polish, Liberon clear or Renaissance wax

1 Cross-hatched area above the egg before removal.

2 Wood removed above the egg.

3 Outline of the head drawn on the side view.

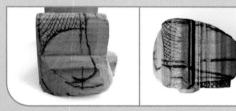

4 Cross-hatched areas above the body and adjacent to the beak to be removed.

Initial steps

The first step is to deal with the egg that sticks out slightly on one side. Draw the egg on the wood in side view. The wood immediately above the egg and the foot is surplus to requirements, so cross-hatch it **1**. Remove this area using a ³⁄₁₆in (5mm) No.5 gouge (this is my most frequently used carving gouge) **2**.

The head

The crane's head is the next part to carve. Draw both the side and end views of the head onto the wood **3**. On the end view, to the left of the head, draw out the shape of the body and cross-hatch the area above it **4**. The beak can be defined against the body by removing the small cross-hatched area next to it using a ³⁄₁₆in (5mm) No.5 gouge.

Afterwards, redraw the beak in side view. Round off the body, neck and head using a ³⁄₁₆in (5mm) No.5 gouge, plus a ¹⁄₄in (6mm) No.9 gouge as this will create a bigger sweep at the bottom of the neck on the end view. Progress has already been made quite quickly; it is already beginning to look like a crane **5**, see overleaf.

5 Good progress has been made quite quickly.

Adding features

Now that the body has been rounded off to create the approximate overall shape of the crane, you can draw the main features, such as eyes, feathers, legs, and the feet onto the side view and the underside. Add centre lines or reference lines in pencil or ink to the carving to ensure that all the features are in the right place in relation to each other. These must stay in the right place throughout the process, otherwise you may spoil your carving with lopsided eyes, for example.

It is always a good idea to use a set of callipers to check dimensions. If in doubt, rub the feature out and redraw it until you are satisfied. As the carving progresses you can redraw any features that have become indistinct.

In the chapter on techniques, I explain how to make and inlay eyes (see pages 42–6). It is important to read this before proceeding with the eyes.

Eyes

Put the eyes in next. For the crane I would use imitation ivory for the white of the eye and buffalo horn for the pupil. You could use holly and ebony instead if these are easier to obtain.

I usually set in the eyes as soon as the carving is sufficiently advanced, as they give focus to the rest of the carving. Another good reason to place the eyes in early is that they cannot be corrected if they are in the wrong place. If the eyes are positioned incorrectly, it is better to abandon the carving at this stage before too much work has been carried out.

Use a small circular cutter in a multi-tool to drill the eye sockets and to make the sockets slightly oval. Then, make an imitation ivory dowel about ¼in (6mm) square in section. With a file shape one end into a small oval until it fits the eye socket exactly. Keep offering the dowel up to the socket and continue filing until it fits exactly.

Place some glue in the socket and push the dowel in, so that it is held firmly in place **6**. If it is loose you have made the dowel too small, so file a bit off the end and repeat the process.

6 The eye before the pupil is inserted.

7 The pupil drawn in ready for inserting.

8 The outline of the feathers carved.

9 Feathers carved on the other wing.

10 Finish carving the feathers and underneath the netsuke.

11 Back of the neck view with some tidying still to be done.

With the same cutter. cut the dowel off about $5/32$in (4mm) from the head, before rounding the eye off with a needle file. Repeat this process for the other eye. Next, cut a very small buffalo-horn dowel about $3/64$in² (1mm²) and round it off to about $1/32$in (0.5mm) to form the pupils **7**. Drill the holes with a $1/32$in (0.5mm) diameter cutter. Finally, shape, glue in and cut off the pupils close to the eyes, before filing them down.

Feathers

After creating the eyes, draw out the feathers ready for carving.

To define the feathers, choose gouges that are the same shape as the individual feathers and push these into the surface. Use a small flat chisel held at a slight angle to trim off the edge of the feathers so they are slightly rounded **8**. You can also try the feathering technique shown in the

photograph **9**. To do this use a $1/16$in (1.5mm) V-tool to make two lines for the spine of the feather with individual vanes coming off each side. At this stage, shape the egg and cut out the toes which hold it, on the side view and underneath. Use a $3/16$in (5mm) No.5 gouge, a $1/16$in (1.5mm) flat chisel and the V-tool to ensure that they are accurately carved. Set in the line between the upper and lower mandibles of the beak by pushing the $3/16$in (5mm) No.5 gouge gently into the beak sufficiently to mark it. Move the chisel along to mark the whole length of the beak.

Using the same chisels, finish carving the other feathers, as well as the other leg and the foot underneath the bird **10**. Shape the back of the neck a little more and clean the whole thing up with fine sandpaper and Micro-Mesh paper **11**. This is as far as you can go without separating the carving from the main block.

12 Cord holes drilled in.   **13** The crane after two sessions of bleaching.

Separation

Separate the crane from the central block before shaping the back with the ¹³⁄₆₄in (5mm) No.5 gouge and carving the tail feathers with the ³⁄₁₆in (1.5mm) V-tool. At this point you should also shape the tail underneath and feather it. Finally, drill the cord holes in the places indicated in the photograph above **12**.

Bleaching

I decided that this particular piece would look more realistic if I bleached the wood to make it lighter. Bleaching raises the grain a little and may mean that some areas will need to be recarved. However, this is not essential and you could leave it in its natural state if you preferred.

Rustins' bleach comes in two bottles of chemicals, as shown on page 66. These must be used in a specific order. With a fine brush paint on the chemical in bottle A and leave it to dry for 20 minutes outside in the sun. Then paint the whole netsuke with the bleach liquid in bottle B and leave it for four hours to dry. Following this, mix a teaspoon of white wine vinegar in 1 pint (568ml) of water and brush over the whole carving to neutralize the bleach, then leave it to dry overnight.

If you find that the grain has become raised in various places the following morning, lightly sand the surface to flatten it again. You can repeat the process if the wood is not light enough **13**.

Final touches

Sand the crane with fine Micro-Mesh to flatten the grain again and to clean it up all over. You may also need to use the ¹⁄₁₆in (1.5mm) V-tool to redefine the existing feather cuts. Go over the whole carving redefining the outline of the egg, the marks on the toes and any other details with gouges and chisels, so it looks sharp and crisp. Put the line between the upper and lower mandible of the beak back in by gently pressing the ³⁄₁₆in (5mm) No.5 chisel into the wood and working your way along the beak.

When all this is done, sand the crane all over with the finest grade Micro-Mesh to prepare it for polishing. Sign your name with a pyrography pen, then polish the netsuke with clear shoe polish. Leave it to soak into the wood, before polishing it off with a clean rag.

The finished netsuke from all angles.

SLEEPING WILD BOAR

This animal is much admired in Japan for its bravery, as it is completely fearless and charges straight at its opponents. To see one sleeping peacefully therefore seems quite a contradiction.

Materials:
- The other half of the limewood block used for carving the netsuke crane

Tools:
Gouges and chisels:
- ³⁄₁₆in (5mm) No.5 gouge
- ¹⁄₁₆in (1.5mm) V-tool
- ³⁄₆₄in (1mm) Dockyard U-gouge
- ¹⁄₄in (3mm) No.5 gouge
- ⁵⁄₆₄in (2mm) Dockyard U-gouge
- ¹⁄₁₆in (1.5mm) No.1 flat chisel

Cutters:
- ³⁄₆₄in (1mm) circular cutter for use in a multi-tool

Miscellaneous
Indian ink:
- Ink with small jar and a clean paint brush

Fine-tipped pen:
- Fine line drawing pen

Abrasives:
- Sandpaper grits from about 100 to 400
- Micro-Mesh paper, 1800 to 12000 grit
- Micro-Mesh stick with 4 grits on the same stick

Finishes:
- Clear polish such as clear shoe polish, Liberon clear or Renaissance wax

① Cross-hatched area above the stone.

② The wood has now been removed.

③ The end view and the side view drawn on.

④ The main part of the body has been rounded and sanded off.

Initial steps

The first step is to deal with the stone on the side of the boar. Cross-hatch the wood above the rock, as shown in the photograph **①**. Then remove it using a ³⁄₁₆in (5mm) No.5 gouge. The second photograph shows how the outline of the stone is revealed after the wood around it has been removed **②**.

Sketching outlines

Draw on the end view, the curve of the body and the snout, and a very preliminary side view of the front legs **③**. The back leg on the opposite side from the stone also has to be drawn in. The top of the body can then be rounded off using the same ³⁄₁₆in (5mm) No.5 gouge. Leave the front legs for the moment as more definition is required.

Adding features

The following photographs show the main part of the body rounded off and sanded to achieve a smooth finish. The smoothness means that it is easier to draw on the main features of the carving. Draw the features as they appear on both sides of the boar as well as the front view **④**.

5 The leaves carved over the boar's back.

6 The front legs redrawn.

7 The bottom of the foot cut off towards the back.

8 View of the underside with the legs in process.

9 The end of this stage with legs and feet roughed out.

10 Tusks and mouth redrawn.

Leaves

Using the ³/₁₆in (5mm) No. 5 gouge, carve the leaves over the boar's back **5**. Press the gouge vertically into the wood along the drawn lines, then carve back to these lines with a near-horizontal cut using the same tool. The leaves should now be slightly raised above the boar's back. The final task at this stage is to carve the rest of the boar's back down to the level adjacent to the leaves.

Eyes and ears

Outline the ears with a ¹/₁₆in (1.5mm) V-tool. Then, using a ³/₆₄in (1mm) Dockyard gouge, carve the hollow inside each ear. A ¹/₈in (3mm) No.5 gouge will fit the curve of the closed eyelid; press the blade into the eyelid line to outline it. Using a ⁵/₆₄in (2mm) Dockyard gouge, carve a semicircle above and below the eyes, and shape the eyelids so that they are both slightly rounded.

Legs and feet

I decided to redraw the front legs slightly differently to those in the original drawing. The trotter end of the leg is now drawn as if folded under the upper leg. The view from underneath shows the corresponding positions of the front and back feet **6**.

To carve the front and back legs you will need a variety of tools: a ³/₁₆in (5mm) No.5 gouge, a ¹/₁₆in (1.5mm) flat chisel, a ¹/₁₆in (1.5mm) V and a ³/₆₄in (1mm) U-gouge. Starting with the front legs, press a ³/₁₆in (5mm) gouge into the wood to follow the curve of the upper leg and press a ¹/₁₆in (1.5mm) flat in to shape the knee. Clear away the wood above these cuts, removing the drawing of the tusks in the process. Press a ¹/₁₆in (1.5mm) flat into the lower part of the leg and move it along in stages to get the curve, then do the same for the trotters. Cut away the bottom of the foot towards the back end of the boar **7**.

11 The tusk in its socket.

12 The tusk has been carved, snout shaped and mouth carved in.

13 View showing snout finally shaped and with nostrils drilled in.

14 Side view before carving the stone.

15 Side view showing the stone after carving.

16 The netsuke with the cord holes drilled.

Turn the netsuke over and press a ³/₁₆in (5mm) No.5 gouge into the inside of the foot, then clear it out **8**. With the same tool, cut out the trotter on the outside of the foot; this should be underneath the upper part of the leg. With a single straight cut using a ¹/₁₆in (1.5mm) V-tool, separate each half of the trotter. Round off the edge of the legs and feet with shallow cuts. Repeat the process for the other feet **9**.

Tusks

Redraw the tusks and outline the mouth ready for carving **10**. The tusks need to be carved with care to ensure that no small bits break off. Carefully press in a ⁵/₆₄in (2mm) Dockyard gouge to mark out the socket where the tusk comes out of the mouth. Next, use a ¹/₈in (3mm) No.5 gouge to outline the bottom and top of the tusks and to clear away the wood each side of the tusk. Repeat the process if necessary to give sufficient depth to the tusks **11**.

Snout

To carve the snout use a ¹/₈in (3mm) No.5 gouge, being careful not to cut into the tusks. When you are satisfied that the snout is the right shape from the front, draw in the mouth and make a series of cuts with a ¹/₁₆in (1.5mm) V-tool to completely outline it **12**. To put the nostrils in the snout use a ³/₆₄in (1mm) diameter burr cutter in a multi-tool. Gently push this in to leave a concave shape at the bottom of each nostril **13**.

The stone

Start with the stone lines next to the body **14**. Press a ³/₁₆in (5mm) No.5 gouge and a ¹/₁₆in (1.5mm) No.1 chisel in on the marked out lines and carve above them to leave around ⁵/₆₄in (2mm) next to the body. Repeat this for each successive layer of stone, working your way to the outside and leaving each layer about ³/₆₄in (1mm) thick. For the stone near the rear end, press the chisels in to make vertical cuts, then cut in at angles to the back and front of these cuts to get the effect that you require **15**.

Adding holes

Use a ³/₆₄in (1mm) diameter burr cutter held firmly in the multi-tool to drill the cord holes underneath. These holes should be drilled in the underside of the body towards the rear **16**. Clean the carving off ready for the next stage.

17 Side view showing stone and leaves.

18 The other side view.

19 The top view showing the leaves.

20 The hair is now almost finished.

21 The dye has been applied and the features inked in.

Last stages

The next series of photographs show the almost completed netsuke. All that is left to do is to carve the hair and separate the carving from the central block **17** **18** **19**.

Hair

In pencil, lightly draw the direction of the hair over the boar's back. Then, take the sharpest $^1/_{16}$in (1.5mm) V-tool you have and make several very shallow cuts close together. Carve in the direction of the pencil lines and slowly cover the back. You may find the area in between the leaves tricky as the cuts will be very short; the only answer is to keep going slowly and carefully. Having a good light source makes these fine details easier to see, so sit in daylight to do this, if possible, or use very good artificial light. It is also important not to rush this stage, as this is the part of the carving that will make or break it **20**.

To finish the hair you will need to separate the boar from the central block. So cut it off, shape the rear end with a $^3/_{16}$in (5mm) No.5 gouge, sand it down and carve the tail. You can then finish drawing and carving the hair all over the boar.

Applying dye

The last stage is to dye the carving with black ink and to sand off the high spots. The aim is to make the hair stand out further and to contrast with the underlying wood. So, water down some black Indian ink and mix it in a small jar. Next, apply clean water using a fine watercolour brush to the surfaces to be dyed. (We are not adding dye to the leaves, the stone, the snout, the trotters, the eyes, the tops of the ears, either tusk, the bottom lip, or the area for the signature underneath, so there is no need to wet them.) After about ten minutes, carefully paint on the dye, avoiding the afore-mentioned areas, then leave it to dry overnight. When the piece is dry, use a fine-line drawing pen to ink in the outline of the eyelids, the joins in the stones, the cleft in the hooves, and anything else that needs more definition **21**.

The following day, sand the netsuke very lightly using 1600 grit Micro-Mesh to take off most of the dye on the high spots. If the dye does not come off easily, use a very sharp scraper to remove it. When you are satisfied that enough of the limewood shows through, sign your work with a pyrography pen, and wax the whole thing with clear wax. Leave the wax to soak in, then polish it with a soft rag.

The finished netsuke from various angles.

HARE

My aim is to carve the netsuke using only four carving tools, to demonstrate the fact that you do not need many small tools to start carving a simple netsuke. (This excludes setting in the eyes, which is done with a burr in a multi-tool.)

Materials:

- Boxwood block for two netsuke 6 x 1⅜ x 1⅜in (150 x 35 x 35mm)
- Buffalo horn, ebony, or African blackwood dowel ¼ x ¼in (6 x 6mm) for the eyes

Tools:

Gouges and chisels:

- ¹/₁₆in (5mm) No.5 gouge
- ¹/₁₆in (1.5mm) No.1 flat chisel
- ¹/₁₆in (1.5mm) Dockyard V-tool
- ¹/₁₆in (1.5mm) Dockyard U-gouge

Cutters:

- ³/₆₄in (1mm) round cutter for drilling the eye sockets

Files:

- Medium-coarse file
- Needle file

Miscellaneous

Sanding wheel:

- For shaping the top and lower sides of the netsuke

Abrasives:

- Sandpaper grits from about 100 to 400 grit
- Micro-Mesh paper, 1800 to 12000 grit
- Micro-Mesh stick with 4 grits on the same stick

Glue:

- Wood glue

Finishes:

- Liberon Black Bison Antique Pine wax

1 Features drawn on the side of the wood.

2 The netsuke rounded off.

3 Main features redrawn on the wood.

4 Features defined on the hare's head.

5 Eyes set in and head roughly carved.

Initial steps

This is the first project carved in my preferred boxwood. First, draw the main features onto the wood **1**. Round off the top and slightly round off the lower sides. This is done using a sanding wheel, although a ³⁄₁₆in (5mm) No.5 gouge is just as good and only slightly slower **2**. Redraw the main features onto the rounded-off surfaces **3**.

Use a ¹⁄₁₆in (1.5mm) gouge to outline the muzzle, mouth, back and sides of the head and the ears **4**. Using a ¹⁄₁₆in (1.5mm) V-tool, rough out the outline of the eyes **5**. Then round off the features with the ³⁄₁₆in (5mm) No.5 gouge. Set in the nose and the sides of the muzzle from the nose to the mouth using the V-tool. Continue to use the ¹⁄₁₆in (1.5mm) gouge to outline the rear and front legs. The body between them should be shaped using the ³⁄₁₆in (5mm) No.5 gouge.

6 The hare ready to receive an eye.

7 The dowel shaped to fit the eye.

8 The dowel being inserted.

9 The dowels have been cut off and rounded.

10 Ears reshaped and shortened.

11 The detail of the feet drawn on.

12 The feet after carving.

The eyes

Drill two eye sockets using a ³⁄₆₄in (1mm) burr in your multi-tool, before enlarging the holes to about ⁵⁄₃₂in (4mm) by running the drill around the inside edge of the holes **6**. Cut some buffalo horn to make a small dowel about ¼in (6mm) square, then round off the end to fit the drilled eye socket **7**. Taper the rounded dowel to ensure a good fit.

Place some glue in the eye socket and insert the dowel **8**. Cut both dowels off about ⅛in (3mm) away from the head and round off the edges with a flat needle file **9**.

The ears

At this point, check the dimensions of the various features on the hare. I found that the ears were far too long, so I shortened them a bit **10**.

The feet

Underneath, draw in the detail of the feet ready for carving **11**. Carve the feet and clean up the area between them **12**. Then mark out the cartouche and the position of the cord holes.

The fur

Sand the whole carving using several grades of fine sandpaper, followed by 1600 grit Micro-Mesh. When it is clean all over, start to carve fur on the head and the body. Lightly draw the hairs on the face in pencil and carve short cuts with a ¹⁄₁₆in (1.5mm) V-tool to indicate short hair **13**. Gradually work your way over the whole head, including the ears, drawing the hair on first before cutting along the drawn lines with a V-tool.

Continue marking out the hairs along the body, making the V-tool cuts fractionally longer to indicate longer hair **14**. Carve the hair towards the rear end until you cannot get at it properly.

13 Top view of head and ears.

14 Side view with the hair carved.

15 Views of the netsuke showing the outline of its tail.

Separation

At this point you need to separate the netsuke from the central block to carve the tail and finish it off. Saw it off and draw in the tail ready for carving **15**.

Finishing touches

Using the ³⁄₁₆in (5mm) No.5 gouge, carve off the waste wood around the tail and then round off the edges with the same tool. Sand the rear end and tail with several grades of fine sandpaper, then finish it off with Micro-Mesh.

With the ¹⁄₁₆in (1.5mm) V-tool finish carving the hair on the back, rear end, tail, and underneath. Drill the cord holes and add your signature in the cartouche with a pyrography pen. Then, go over the whole piece with fine grades of Micro-Mesh, finishing with 16,000 grit.

To finish, apply a slightly darker wax polish, for example Liberon Black Bison Antique Pine wax, leave for a few minutes then polish with a clean rag. Some of the wax will remain in the low spots of the V-tool cuts, providing contrast and ensuring that the fur stands out.

The finished netsuke from various angles.

DIVING FROG

This netsuke will also be carved in boxwood and is based on a diving frog made by Fabergé in jade and diamonds. This time however, I thought I would carve it, as far as possible, with power tools.

Materials:

- The second half of the boxwood block
- Buffalo horn, ebony or African blackwood for the eyes

Tools:

Gouges and chisels:

- $\frac{1}{16}$in (1.5mm) Dockyard V-tool
- $\frac{1}{16}$in (1.5mm) Dockyard gouge
- $\frac{1}{16}$in (1.5mm) flat chisel

Cutters:

- $\frac{1}{4}$in (6mm) round
- $\frac{3}{16}$in (5mm) elliptical
- $\frac{5}{32}$in (4mm) tapered
- $\frac{5}{64}$in (2mm) round
- $\frac{5}{32}$in (4mm) reverse cone
- $\frac{5}{64}$in (2mm) pointed taper

Miscellaneous

Sanding wheel:

- For shaping the top and lower sides of the netsuke

Abrasives:

- Sandpaper, medium and fine grit
- Micro-Mesh paper, 1800 to 12000 grit
- Micro-Mesh stick with 4 grits on the same stick

Glue:

- Wood glue

Finishes:

- Clear polish such as clear shoe polish, Liberon clear or Renaissance wax

1 Area to be removed shown in cross-hatch.

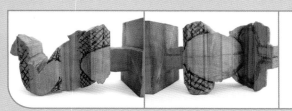

2 The wood has been removed around the legs.

Initial steps

First, draw the main features onto the wood, cross-hatching the areas where the wood is to be removed **1**. Remove the cross-hatched areas around the front legs with a ¼in (6mm) circular burr. Concentrate on one side at a time, keeping the speed to about a third of full power, and gradually cut the hatched wood away until it reaches the main body.

Legs

Cut around the back legs where they join the body, then the ends of the legs near the feet, before cutting away the wood above the front legs **2**.

As the cutters remove wood quickly, it is easy to cut too deep, so be careful when you are getting close to other features. The burr cutters used in the multi-tool machine are shown on pages 27–8.

If this is the first time you have done any power carving, take your time. If you find the multi-tool difficult to hold after a while, take a break and exercise your fingers.

3 Underneath view showing the area to be removed.

4 View of the back with the eyes drawn on.

5 Looking from the feet end.

6 The outline shown from underneath.

7 Wood carved around and between the eyes.

8 The eye socket and mouth drawn in.

All the hatched areas should now have been removed, except for the area between the frog's back legs **3**.

Still using the 1/4in (6mm) cutter, drill through the hatched area between the back legs. Start from the top of the frog and work down towards the underside; this will make it easier to ensure that the drilled hole comes out in the hatched area on the underside. Once you are through, enlarge the hole with the 1/4in (6mm) cutter, until you get close to the edge of the hatched area. At this point, change to the 5/64in (2mm) round cutter to cut up to the line more carefully **4** **5** **6**.

Eyes and mouth

Using the 5/64in (2mm) cutter, cut between the eyes on the top of the frog until the area between them is level with the body in front and behind. With the same cutter, cut round the eyes on the side view, then roughly shape them **7**. Using the 5/32in (4mm) tapered cutter, smooth the surface between the eyes and round off any sharp edges. Work the frog all over until it begins to form its rounded body shape.

Draw in the eye sockets and the mouth **8**. Then drill out the eyes with a 5/64in (2mm) round cutter. With the 5/32in (4mm) reverse cone, tilted so that only the edge comes in contact with the wood, carefully put the mouth line in.

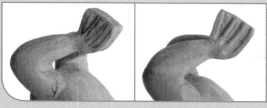

9 Toes drawn and roughly carved.

10 Lines drawn around the mouth.

11 Both eyes have now been fitted.

12 The frog separated from the main block.

Back feet

Next, draw the toes on the back feet and use a ⁵⁄₆₄in (2mm) round cutter to cut gaps between the toes **9**. If the back feet are still too thick, make them thinner with a ⁵⁄₃₂in (4mm) tapered cutter, redraw them and repeat the first step.

Facial features

Draw in the area in front of the eyes and hatch in this area **10**. This will be hollowed out to make a shallow depression leading up to the nostrils. Lastly, mark the lines above and below the mouth to outline it.

Remove the hatched area in front of the eyes with a ⁵⁄₆₄in (2mm) round cutter, then cut along the lines above and below the mouth with a ¹⁄₁₆in (1.5mm) V-tool to outline it. Use the V-tool instead of the cutter in order to get better control and a finer cut.

To put in the eyes, use imitation ivory for the whites, followed by buffalo-horn pupils. A more detailed description of making eyes is given on pages 42–4 **11**.

Separation

To complete the front end of the netsuke carving, including the front feet, remove the frog from its main block **12**. Make sure that the base is flat, yet cut with a slight upward incline from back to front, to throw the weight forward so the frog looks as if it is diving into water.

13 Underside details drawn on.

14 The feet have been carved.

15 Details have been drawn in.

16 The additional features have now been carved and the frog is almost finished.

Front feet

At the front of the underside draw on the front feet and the frog's facial features as shown **13**. Carve the feet with a ³⁄₆₄in (1mm) cutter in the multi-tool, then the area below the mouth with a ¹⁄₁₆in (1.5mm) V-tool and a ¹⁄₁₆in (1.5mm) Dockyard gouge **14**. I decided to do this using carving chisels rather than power tools, as this gives you greater control. It would be devastating to overcut with a power tool and ruin the carving at this late stage.

Additional features

Looking back at my research, I noticed that there is a ridge down each side of the back of the frog, from the nose right down to the rear end. I drew these on the carving as shown **15**, then carved them with a ¹⁄₁₆in (1.5mm) V-tool. The next step is to clear the areas at each side of the V-cuts with the flat ¹⁄₁₆in (1.5mm) chisel before carving the eardrum behind the eyes and the outline of the nostrils **16**. Finally, sand, sign and polish the carving.

The finished netsuke from various angles.

Mandarin Duck

The beautiful and colourful Mandarin duck originally comes from the Far East, and was often carved into netsuke by the Japanese. Here the duck is carved in cherry wood and inlaid with colourful feathers to illustrate the process of inlaying.

Materials:

- Cherry block, 6 x 1⅜ x 1⅜in (150 x 35 x 35mm)
- Buffalo horn, ebony or African blackwood to make dowels
- Imitation ivory, holly or real ivory if you prefer
- Yew or yew veneer
- Coloured resin or paua shell

Tools:

Gouges and chisels:
- ³⁄₁₆in (5mm) No.5 gouge
- ¼in (6mm) No.9 gouge
- ¹⁄₁₆in (1.5mm) dockyard V-tool
- ⅛in (3mm) No.1 flat chisel
- ¹⁄₁₆in (1.5mm) No.1 flat chisel
- ⁵⁄₃₂in (4mm) No.9 gouge

Cutters:
- ³⁄₆₄in (1mm) circular cutter
- ¹⁄₁₆in (1.5mm) circular cutter
- ⁵⁄₆₄in (2mm) circular cutter
- ⁵⁄₃₂in (4mm) tapered cutter
- ⁵⁄₆₄in (2mm) parallel-sided cutter

Files:
- Medium-coarse files
- Needle files

Miscellaneous

Abrasives:
- Sandpaper from 100 to 400 grit
- Micro-Mesh paper, 1800 to 12000 grit.
- Micro-Mesh stick with 4 grits on the same stick.

Glue:
- Wood glue

Finishes:
- Clear polish such as clear shoe polish, Liberon clear wax or Renaissance wax.

1 Views of both sides showing the cross-hatched areas to be removed.

2 The wood in these areas has now been removed.

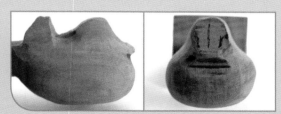

3 Netsuke sanded smooth.

Initial steps

Draw the outline onto a piece of cherry wood and cross-hatch the areas to be removed **1**. Using a ³⁄₁₆in (5mm) No.5 gouge, remove the hatched areas to give the approximate shape of the Mandarin duck **2**. Sand the carving to get a smooth outline ready for drawing in the main features again **3**. The enlarged drawing on the right shows the parts to be inlaid, together with options for the materials that can be used.

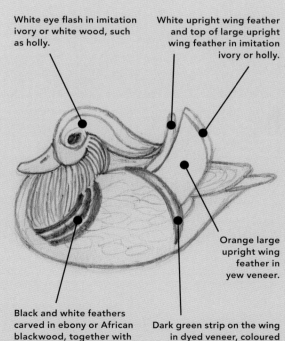

White eye flash in imitation ivory or white wood, such as holly.

White upright wing feather and top of large upright wing feather in imitation ivory or holly.

Orange large upright wing feather in yew veneer.

Black and white feathers carved in ebony or African blackwood, together with imitation ivory or holly.

Dark green strip on the wing in dyed veneer, coloured resin or paua shell.

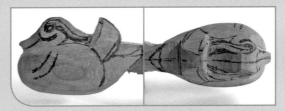

④ Main features redrawn on the netsuke.

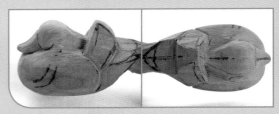

⑤ Beak and tuft behind the head carved.

⑥ Enlarged front and back views of feathers.

The Head

Redraw the main features, then start to carve the beak and tuft at the back of the head ④. Use a ¼in (6mm) No.9 gouge to mark in the curve at the front lower part of the head and a ¹⁄₁₆in (1.5mm) V-tool to continue this line from the front of the head over the top of the bill to meet the similar line from the other side. Using a ⅛in (3mm) No.1 chisel, round off the head into this cut and carve the side of the beak, cutting in at the head end and running the cut out towards the front of the bill. Repeat this for both sides of the head and the bill until it looks right. Remember that the front of the head tapers towards the beak and that the eyes are angled slightly forwards.

Next, carve the tuft at the back of the head which tapers into the middle of the back between the two large upright feathers each side of the wings ⑤. Use a ¹⁄₁₆in (1.5mm) No.1 chisel to push a cut straight into the bottom part of the side feather. Then use a ⅛in (3mm) No.1 chisel to cut from the head towards the first cut to remove a small wedge of wood. At the same time clean up the bottom of the cut by the wing. Repeat this several times for both sides until the tuft tapers up to the drawn line as shown.

In real life the upright wing feathers do not touch each other, but you can use some artistic licence, as I did, and make them touch at the top to add strength. Thin the feathers at the side with a ³⁄₁₆in (5mm) No.5 gouge, then pierce between the wings with a ⁵⁄₆₄in (2mm) cutter in the multi-tool so that the cord can pass through ⑥. Enlarge this hole using a ¹⁄₁₆in (1.5mm) chisel.

7 One eye flash cut out and the other one drawn ready for shaping.

8 Recess removed for the eye-flash socket.

9 Imitation ivory let in but not yet filed down.

10 Eye flash filed down to the side of the head.

11 Eye socket drawn on, then drilled.

Eye flash

The first piece of inlay is the eye flash, which needs to be drawn out on each side of the head. Inlay it with imitation ivory about $\frac{1}{8}$in (3mm) thick to accommodate the curve of the head. Cut a small piece of imitation ivory and draw the eye flash on it in pencil, checking the dimensions and shape **7**.

Cut out the eye flash with a $\frac{5}{32}$in (4mm) tapered cutter to create the rough shape of the eye flash. Recess the eye flash on each side of the head by marking the outline of the eye flash with a $\frac{3}{16}$in (5mm) No.5 gouge, a $\frac{5}{32}$in (4mm) No.9 gouge and a $\frac{1}{16}$in (1.5mm) chisel **8**. Mark the outline by pressing the gouges and chisels into the wood to fit the outline of the eye flash. Use a $\frac{1}{16}$in (1.5mm) No.1 chisel to cut from the inside of the eye flash towards the outline cuts and carefully remove the recess to about $\frac{3}{64}$in (1mm) deep; repeat the outlining process as necessary.

Start to fit the imitation ivory eye flash into the recess by offering it up, noting where it doesn't fit, then filing bits off with a needle file **9**. Keep doing this until the eye flash fits well. Some of the ivory will stick out above the surface, but this can be filed down **10**.

Glue the ivory piece into the recess and repeat the process for the other side of the head. This is a time-consuming process, but as always the aim is to make the piece as good as possible.

Draw on the eye sockets and drill them out with a $\frac{5}{64}$in (2mm) round burr cutter in the multi-tool. Drill straight into the imitation ivory, but be careful not to enlarge the hole **11**.

12 Yew upright wing feather glued in place.

13 Thin sliver of imitation ivory.

14 Upright yew and imitation ivory feathers glued on.

15 Sliver of ivory glued on top of yew feather.

16 Recess cut below yew feather for green stripe.

Feathers

The next stage is to add colour to the wing feathers. On a Mandarin duck the large back part is orange and the narrow front part is white. Therefore cut some yew, which is an orange colour, to about ⁵⁄₆₄in (2mm) thick, then shape the large back part and glue it onto the existing cherry surface **12**. When the glue is completely dry, thin it down with a ³⁄₁₆in (5mm) No.5 gouge.

For the front upright feather cut a thin sliver of imitation ivory and roughly shape it using a ⁵⁄₃₂in (4mm) tapered cutter in the multi-tool **13**. File this down to the correct shape with needle files, concentrating on getting the back of the front feather to fit closely against the yew feather, and glue this in front of the yew feather **14**. It will stick out beyond its proper shape, but it can be filed down when the glue has dried. Repeat the process for the other wing.

Next, cut thin slivers of imitation ivory to fit the top of the yew feathers. The important thing is to make the shape match the curve on top of the yew feather by offering it up to see if it fits and filing it down until it does. Do not worry about the top surface as the final shaping can take place when the piece has been glued on and is really dry **15**.

To attain the green stripe at the back of the wing, draw and cut a recess in the back of the wing **16**. Mark the lines by pressing a ³⁄₁₆in (5mm) No.5 gouge into the lines of the curve, and clearing it out with a ¹⁄₁₆in (1.5mm) flat chisel.

17 The paua shell for the green feathers.

18 Shaped paua shell offered up.

19 The shell has now been glued, filed and polished.

20 One eye in and the dowel in the other eye ready for cutting off.

21 The eye rounded off and the ruff carved.

Safety note:
Paua shell dust is poisonous, so always wear a mask when cutting it.

For the green stripe itself, cut paua shell using a ⁵⁄₆₄in (2mm) almost parallel-sided cutter. Cut two smaller pieces from the large shell and from each make a crescent-shaped inlay **17**. I strongly suggest that you use a mask whilst cutting the paua shell as it is poisonous when carved.

Offer the paua shell up to the recess and file it down until it fits, then put glue in the recess and place the shell in **18**. As the body curves inwards towards the base, a small part of the shell may stick out. If it does, push it until it breaks, so that it fits the bottom part of the recess. Fill over the joint when the glue has dried. This will be masked by dark hard wax in the finishing process. Repeat the process for the other side of the duck. Finally, file off any sharp bits before going over it all with a Micro-Mesh stick, starting at the coarse grade and finishing off with the finest. You will see the colour emerge from the shell **19**.

Eyes

Put the eyes in next. Start by cutting a small piece of buffalo horn on the bandsaw, then round off one end on the sanding wheel to the approximate diameter of the eye. Using a file, round the dowel with a slight taper towards the head. Keep filing until it is fits well in the eye socket. Glue one eye in and cut it off about ⁵⁄₆₄in (2mm) from the head with a ¹⁄₁₆in (1.5mm) cutter, before repeating the process for the other eye **20**.

When the glue has fully dried, file the eyes to a dome shape with a flat needle file **21**. When you are happy with the shape, polish the eyes with a Micro-Mesh stick until they take on a good shine; this will give the impression of sight to the eyes.

Photograph by Paul Reader.

22 Colourful Mandarin duck.

Modifications

At this stage in the carving, a woodcarver friend of mine who saw what I was carving, gave me a fantastic photograph that he had taken of a Mandarin duck **22**. This was quite different from the drawings I had been working from and meant that I needed to modify the carving slightly. It is quite acceptable to adapt your design as you progress through the carving to improve it.

It is not possible to reproduce all the fantastic colours in a netsuke carving, but perhaps by bringing out the main features, it will be a close resemblance.

Ruff and chest feathers

The ruff of feathers each side of the head is the next feature to carve. Draw the extent of the ruff and run a ¹⁄₁₆in (1.5mm) V-tool along the line. Clear away the outside of the curve with a ¹⁄₁₆in (1.5mm) flat chisel. In pencil, draw the feather lines on and carefully carve them in with a ¹⁄₁₆in (1.5mm) V-tool. In retrospect, putting in the black and white inlay next to it first would have protected the ruff when putting in the inlay.

To inlay the black and white feathers on each side of the chest, set African blackwood into the body of the duck, then inlay it with white imitation ivory. Try this on a test piece first to avoid ruining the carving at this late stage. Using a ³⁄₆₄in (1mm) cutter, cut two slots close together in the blackwood. Thin down slices of imitation ivory using a sanding wheel and file them to fit in the slots **23**.

23 Slices of ivory in the blackwood test piece.

24 Shaped piece for each side of the chest.

25 Outline of insert drawn out.

26 Recess cut out for the blackwood insert.

27 Views of the first insert before filing down.

28 Imitation ivory in the first slot.

29 The blackwood insert with the imitation ivory inlaid.

When you are satisfied cut a piece of African blackwood about 2 x ¼ x ¼in (50 x 6 x 6mm). In white pencil draw the general shape of the group of feathers. Shape this with a ⁵⁄₃₂in (4mm) tapered cutter in the multi-tool, making sure that you leave a piece to hold on to. When you have the right shape, saw it in half so you have the same shape for each side of the chest **24**.

On each side of the chest draw out the shape of the blackwood insert **25**. Press a ³⁄₁₆in (5mm) No.5 gouge and a ¹⁄₁₆in (1.5mm) flat chisel into the outline then clear out the wood within the outline to create a recess **26**. This has to go fairly deep, so that the insert can absorb the shape of the chest.

Separate the blackwood from its handle before offering it up to the recess, filing and trimming until it fits. It is best to do this over an empty box,

so that if you drop it you will be able to find it again. If it landed on my workshop floor, I would never find it again! Glue the piece in and leave it for 24 hours before filing it down **27**. Do this carefully to ensure that you do not scratch the adjacent surface.

When the insert has been filed down, finish it off by going through the grades of paper on a Micro-Mesh stick until it really shines. Next cut the first slot for the imitation ivory insert; this should be about ⅛in (3mm) deep. File a piece of imitation ivory until it fits the length and width of the slot. Glue it in and leave it to dry **28**. Once it is dry, file it down to the surface of the blackwood and repeat the process **29**.

The next task is to draw and carve the ruff, as well as the blackwood and ivory inlays on the other side of the bird.

30 Beak recarved with the nostrils put in.

31 The outline of the wings and feathers defined.

32 The carving is now separated from the central block.

33 View of the rearmost wing feathers drawn in.

34 The rearmost wing feathers rounded off and the tail set in.

35 Wing and tail feathers carved in.

Definition

At this point I decided that the beak on my carving was too long and too wide. If you find that this is the case, trim it down with a ³⁄₁₆in (5mm) No.5 gouge before putting the nostrils in with a ¹⁄₁₆in (1.5mm) V-tool **30**.

Define the outline of the upper and lower parts of the wings with a ¹⁄₁₆in (1.5mm) V-tool **31**. Outline just a small number of feathers, as on the real bird the wing feathers are hardly noticeable as individual feathers.

Separation

Separate the duck from its central block, so that you can draw the rearmost wing feathers and tail feathers before carving them **32**.

Then draw in the outline of the wing feathers, carve them using a ¹⁄₁₆in (1.5mm) V-tool and shape each wing. One of the wings should overlap the other slightly **33**.

The wings should now be outlined and rounded off, with the tail feathers set back to just below the wing feathers. Finally, round off the body below the tail and add your signature **34** **35**.

The finished Mandarin duck from various angles.

BAT

The fruit bat is the last in the series of stage-by-stage netsuke carvings, and will be carved in cherry. It is based on a traditional netsuke carving of a bat which was carved in ivory and various woods. This one is about to open its wings to fly.

Materials:

- The second half of the cherry block
- ⅛in x ⅛in (3 x 3mm) Buffalo horn, ebony or African blackwood dowel for the eyes

Tools:

Gouges and chisels:

- ³⁄₁₆in (5mm) No.5 gouge
- ¼in (6mm) No.9 gouge
- ¹⁄₁₆in (1.5mm) Dockyard V-tool
- ¹⁄₁₆in (1.5mm) Dockyard gouge

Cutters:

- ³⁄₆₄in (1mm) circular cutter
- ⁵⁄₃₂in (4mm) circular cutter

Files:

- Medium-coarse file
- Needle files

Miscellaneous

Abrasives:

- Sandpaper from about 100 to 400 grit
- Micro-Mesh paper, 1800 to 12000 grit
- Micro-Mesh stick with four grits on the same stick

Glue:

- Wood glue

Finishes:

- Clear polish such as clear shoe polish, Liberon clear wax or Renaissance wax

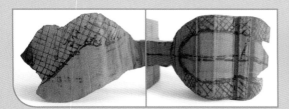 

1 The cross-hatched area above the wing is to be removed.

2 Views showing the wood removed above the wings.

3 Features drawn with the head partly rounded off.

4 The eyes set in and the face shaped.

Initial steps

Draw the design onto the wood, cross-hatch the area above the wings **1** and remove it back to the body using a ³⁄₁₆in (5mm) No.5 gouge and a ¼in (6mm) No.9 gouge **2**.

Features

Round off the top of the body, then mark in the eyes and the ears **3**.

Set in the ears and carve round the eye area. Shape the face and put in the very small eyes with buffalo-horn dowels **4**. This is described in more detail on pages 42–4.

5 Views showing the tapered wings.

6 The cross-hatched areas from underneath.

7 The back legs and tail drawn in.

8 The progression of the underside.

Taper the wings from the base towards the top of the wings near the body, using a ³⁄₁₆in (5mm) No.5 gouge **5**.

Underside

Turn the bat over and cross-hatch the area to be carved away on the underside, between the wings and the body **6**.

Ensure that you do not carve too much away before dealing with the back legs and tail. Draw these features in and clarify the whole area as shown **7** **8**.

Wings

Draw out the wings on each side of the bat **9**. With a ¹⁄₁₆in (1.5mm) V-tool, cut along the finger lines on the wings, before clearing away. Use a ¹⁄₁₆in (1.5mm) U-gouge between the fingers where they are close together and a ³⁄₁₆in (5mm) No. 5 gouge above the top finger. Press a ³⁄₁₆in (5mm) No.5 gouge along the edges of the bat's fingers to outline them **10**.

9 The wings drawn in.

10 The finger lines along the wings carved

11 Adding definition to the bat's face.

12 Hair on the head carved.

13 The holes and the reserve located.

14 Carving the hair underneath.

15 Feet shaped ready for drawing in the toes.

Definition

Carve the nose and mouth with a ¹⁄₁₆in (1.5mm) V-tool, rounding off around the nose and mouth with a fine file **11**. This is also a good time to file between the fingers on the wings, around the ears and the underside of the body.

Hair

The hair on the face and back is the next area to carve. Draw the general direction of the hair on a small area, then carve this using a ¹⁄₁₆in (1.5mm) V-tool to create short strokes, before moving on to the next bit **12**.

Before carving the hair on the underside of the body, draw in the reserve for the signature and the locations of the cord holes. Whilst drawing on the underside, mark in the positions of the fingers on the inside of the wings ready for outlining with a ¹⁄₁₆in (1.5mm) V-tool **13**.

Next, start to carve the hair on the underside as well as the fingers on the inside of the wings **14**. Outline the join between the body and wing on the underside by pushing a ³⁄₁₆in (5mm) No.5 gouge into the wood along the join to mark it in.

Legs and feet

Before you finish carving the hair on the belly of the bat, finish carving the legs and feet. The feet should have a hollow on the underside which should be carved before drawing in the toes and carving them with a ¹⁄₁₆in (1.5mm) V-tool. The underside of the feet should be shaped, so they are ready for drawing in the toes **15**.

16 The toes drawn in.

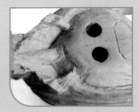

17 The toes have now been carved.

18 Back view of bat separated from block.

19 End of wings and tail carved.

20 Underside of tail finished.

21 Toes carved on the tops of the feet.

Draw on the toes and carve them **16** **17**. They will be easier to see if some dark wax is applied to the feet. Also, drill the cord holes with a ⁵⁄₃₂in (4mm) round cutter and interconnect them; for further details on this see page 69.

Separation

Before you carve the hair on the underside, separate the bat from the block with a coping saw **18**. Then shape the tail on the outside with a ³⁄₁₆in (5mm) No.5 gouge and finish carving the inside **19** **20**. Finally, finished carving the detail on the toes on the tops of the feet **21**.

Finishing touches

All that's left to do is to carve the hair on the underside of the body, sand it down to tidy up all the loose ends, sign it and polish it. Wax the finished carving with Liberon Antique Pine wax. This lies in the bottom of the hairline cuts and makes the hair show up better. When you polish the carving the high spots shine, bringing it to life.

The finished bat, shown from various angles.

AUTHOR'S COLLECTION

CREATE YOUR OWN NETSUKE

Before starting to carve a netsuke, it is advisable to have a clear picture in your mind of the object you are going to carve, including all the details.

Until you gain in confidence, copying another netsuke is ideal as you have a three-dimensional object with all the detail to look at. Genuine pieces can be expensive, but resin-cast copies or wooden reproductions and tagua nut carvings can all be purchased very cheaply. Alternatively you can create drawings, especially if you wish to design your own netsuke. I have a hardback book, solely for my ideas and drawings of netsuke which I would like to carve.

On the following pages I have reproduced 23 of my own netsuke projects. Wildlife carvings are where my interest lies, therefore all the pieces are of wildlife subjects. Many of the designs are based on traditional Japanese netsuke subjects, others are based on modern pieces. They are predominately *katabori* netsuke, those that have been carved in the round.

For each one I have included my original drawings and several photographs of the finished piece taken from various angles. In some cases, adjustments have been made during the carving process, so the finished item is not exactly the same as the original drawing. Hopefully the combination of drawings and photographs will give you enough reference to be able to carve one yourself. If you prefer, you can also make a model of the netsuke to give you a better idea of how it should look before you start to carve.

I also briefly mention the inspiration or the story behind each design, the materials I used, and any particular techniques that were used in the project, with links back to the relevant technique pages providing further explanation. I have also provided precise measured dimensions for each project.

Tools used in all the projects

The full range of tools are shown on pages 18–19. The most commonly used tools in the following projects are:

- 1/16in (1.5mm) U-gouge
- 5/32in (4mm) No.9 gouge
- 1/16in (1.5mm) V-tool
- 1/4in (6mm) No.7 gouge
- 3/16in (5mm) No.5 gouge
- 1/16in (1.5mm) No.1 chisel
- 3/32in (2.5mm) No.7 gouge
- 1/8in (3mm) No.10 gouge
- 1/4in (6mm) No.9 gouge
- *Ukibori* tool
- Bradawl tool

Simple ●
Moderate ●
Advanced ●

OWL

Inspiration

This is my interpretation of a classical Japanese owl netsuke. The owl has its wings hunched up over its head in an aggressive manner in order to try to make it look fierce. The sketch of the netsuke changed slightly from the original. The grain is running up the carving, therefore the small feet as shown in the drawing would almost certainly have broken off. The feet were therefore carved so that they are more substantial. To add a bit of humour there is also a mouse hiding behind the owl's feet.

Technique

I decided to carve this piece from boxwood, inlaying its eyes with ivory and buffalo horn. After carving and sanding the netsuke, I stained it with coffee-brown dye. By sanding it off afterwards, I ensured that the dye remained in the low spots in the feathering while the natural boxwood colour shows up on the high spots. Finally, I added two cord holes underneath.

Dimensions: Width: 1⅝in (42mm) Height: 2in (50mm) Depth: 1⁹⁄₁₆in (40mm)

Materials

• Boxwood, pear or applewood
• Beads, amber or imitation ivory and buffalo horn
  for the eyes

Links

• Inlaying eyes (see pages 42–6)
• Feathering (see page 52)
• Drilling cord holes (see page 69)

● **Simple**
● Moderate
● Advanced

DORMOUSE

Inspiration

I regularly work at Wakehurst Place, the country garden in West Sussex of The Royal Botanic Gardens, Kew as a volunteer guide. There we have hazel dormice which are an endangered species in the UK. We do all we can to produce a habitat that will enable them to thrive, including erecting hibernating boxes in the winter. One of the wardens took an award-winning photograph of three hibernating dormice. This prompted me to draw and carve a netsuke dormouse, with its long tail curved over its head.

Technique

I carved this netsuke out of boxwood and, after the general shaping of the body and the tail, inserted the buffalo-horn eyes. I spent some time drawing the hair onto the wood in order to achieve two different effects: fluffy hair on the tail and short hair on the body. Medium-length curving cuts were made on the tail and very short straight cuts on the body using a $1/16$in (1.5mm) V-tool. Finally, I stained the piece with coffee-coloured fabric dye and sanded off the high spots to leave the dye in the low spots.

Dimensions: Width: 1⅜in (35mm) Height: 1⅜in (35mm) Depth: 1³⁄₁₆in (30mm)

Materials

• Boxwood

• Buffalo horn for the eyes

Links

• Carving short hair (see page 50)

• Inlaying eyes (see pages 42–6)

HEDGEHOG

Inspiration

One autumn, I saw a hedgehog wandering around the garden and assumed that it would soon be building a nest for hibernating during the long winter. I thought it would make an unusual netsuke carving subject, so I sketched this one gathering up leaves. I decided to carve it in boxwood on a base covered in oak leaves to make it look as though it was gathering up leaves with its front feet.

Technique

I tried to make the back of the hedgehog appear prickly by carving short, straight lines with a $\frac{1}{16}$in (1.5mm) V-tool. Next, I sparrow-pecked the gaps between the oak leaves to make them stand out further. The netsuke was then waxed with an antique pine wax, which is fairly dark. The wax lies in the low spots while the high spots polish off to a shine, providing contrast. There was enough room underneath to sign and date the netsuke and to put in the cord holes.

Dimensions: Width: 1⅞in (48mm) Height: 1⅝in (42mm) Depth: 1³⁄₁₆in (30mm)

Materials

- Boxwood
- Buffalo horn for the eyes

Links

- Carving short hair (see page 50)
- Sparrow pecking (see page 49)
- Inlaying eyes (see pages 42–6)
- Drilling cord holes (see page 69)

TOADSTOOLS

Inspiration

Japanese netsuke carvers make many types of toadstools in many different materials, and usually in small groups. I saw a small, compact ivory group that I particularly liked in a book. It was so compact and tactile that I was eager to have a go at making my own variation in wood. In order to tie the group together, I had to curve the outer stems inwards at their base to join the central and largest toadstool.

Technique

I sketched the group of toadstools, then carved them from a piece of Tasmanian Huon pinewood. To avoid getting confused early on, I drew all the toadstools out on the surface of the wood in each view. Once I started carving, the position of each toadstool quickly became clear. There was no need to create separate cord holes as the holes between the individual fungi were large enough for a cord to pass through.

Dimensions: Width: 1¼in (32mm) Height: 1³⁄₁₆in (30mm) Depth: 1⅜in (35mm)

Materials
• Boxwood, but could also use many other woods

Links
• Carving gills underneath, same as carving hair (see page 50)

● **Simple**
● Moderate
● Advanced

BUMBLEBEE

Inspiration

This is one of the few *manju* netsuke I have carved, and unfortunately there is a very sad story to it. A good friend was very ill and asked me to carve a netsuke of a bumblebee for her daughter. As a child her daughter would take a plastic one in to exams as a good-luck charm but it had become lost. As soon as I had finished it, I took the piece to her in the hospice, and she gave it to her daughter. She immediately realized the significance of it and there were tears all round. My friend sadly died a couple of days later. At the funeral her daughter told me that she had the netsuke in her pocket.

Technique

This piece is carved in boxwood. I carved the wood away from the bumblebee into the bowl of the rose, leaving the wings up to rest on the edge of the rose petals. I carved the hair on the back of the body with a $\frac{1}{16}$in (1.5mm) V-tool, making short cuts to resemble the short hair. I inlaid the eyes with buffalo horn, and stained the legs and black bits on the back with black ink, being careful not to go into the yellow bands on the bee's back. I carved the veins on the wings with a $\frac{1}{16}$in (1.5mm) V-tool and inked them in. The two cord holes were drilled in the back.

Dimensions: Width: 1⁹⁄₁₆in (40mm) Height: 1⁹⁄₁₆in (40mm) Depth: ²³⁄₃₂in (18mm)

Materials

• Boxwood
• Buffalo horn for the eyes
• Indian ink for the legs, back and veins

Links

• Carving short hair (see page 50)
• Inlaying eyes (see pages 42–6)
• Drilling cord holes (see page 69)

● **Simple**
● Moderate
● Advanced

NAUTILUS

Inspiration

I am quite fascinated by these strange ocean creatures. They are very similar to an octopus except with a shell for protection. Nautilus drift in the warm open oceans and can change their depth at will. They also have good eyesight and catch passing prey by shooting their tentacles out in front of their shell. When I saw a fantastic nautilus netsuke carved by Sue Wraight, I was so impressed with its compactness and colouring that I was inspired into have a go at making one myself. This gave me experience in dyeing areas close together.

Technique

To add the final details to the carving I used the *ukibori* technique on the area above the eyes, then inlaid each eye with buffalo horn and inked in the curved sliver below the pupils. I painted watercolour masking fluid onto the surface of the shell, leaving the areas to be painted exposed. The next step was to paint the exposed surface with warm water, and after a few minutes apply the dye. I left the netsuke to dry overnight before peeling off the masking fluid. Finally, I dyed the carapace and the areas around the tentacles. When the piece was dry, I sanded off the high spots and polished it with clear wax polish.

Dimensions: Width: 1¾in (45mm) Height: 1⁹⁄₁₆in (40mm) Depth: ⅞in (22mm)

Materials

• Boxwood
• Buffalo horn for the eyes
• Masking fluid
• Dye and black ink

Links

• Use of masking fluid and dyeing (see pages 62–5)
• *Ukibori* bumps (see pages 48–9)
• Inlaying eyes (see pages 42–6)
• Drilling cord holes (see page 69)

RABBIT

Inspiration

The rabbit is a subject popular with early Japanese netsuke carvers, who would carve it either singly or in groups. A rabbit scratching to get rid of a flea quickly became a favourite netsuke subject of mine. I like the humour that this brings to the netsuke, as the expression on the rabbit's face shows relief from the irritating flea. This is quite a simple carving and should therefore be one of the first you attempt.

Technique

I chose to carve this piece in holly. I cut the netsuke out in both directions, carved it, then inlaid buffalo horn for the eyes. After sanding and then finishing the piece with Micro-Mesh, I waxed it with clear shoe polish. When this was rubbed off and polished it produced a lovely sheen. I decided not to carve the hair, but to leave the surface smooth instead.

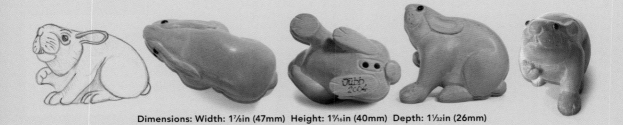

Dimensions: Width: 1⅞in (47mm) Height: 1⁹⁄₁₆in (40mm) Depth: 1¹⁄₃₂in (26mm)

Materials

- Holly, boxwood or other woods

Links

- Inlaying eyes (see pages 42–6)
- Drilling cord holes (see page 69)

● **Simple**
● Moderate
● Advanced

PLATYPUS

Inspiration

At the end of a long and enjoyable walk in a nature reserve near Canberra, Australia, I stopped to watch a platypus surfacing in a lake. I couldn't see much, just the occasional ripple on the surface where it had come up to breathe. Some years later, my brother brought a small bronze of a sleeping platypus back from Australia, which he loaned to me as reference for a netsuke.

The platypus is a strange animal: it has a beak like a duck, it has soft fur all over, webbed feet and sharp claws. It has a tail shaped a bit like that of a beaver, except that it is covered in fur. It also lays eggs and suckles its young.

Dimensions: Width: 1¾in (45mm) Height: 1⁷⁄₁₆in (37mm) Depth: 1⁷⁄₁₆in (37mm)

Materials

• Boxwood
• Black ink for the eyes

Links

• Carving short hair (see page 50)
• Drilling cord holes (see page 69)

Technique

I drew the platypus out in several directions on paper. I shaped a ball in boxwood to fit the largest dimension of the netsuke and drew the platypus on it in side view. I carved its outline shape, then repeated the process for the front view. When the shaping was complete, I carved the head, beak, legs, feet, and tail. Following this, I sanded the piece all over before carving the hair with short cuts using a ¹⁄₁₆in (1.5mm) V-tool. I also inked in between the upper and lower eyelids to give the head some focus. I waxed the netsuke with darker polish, which accentuates the fur when polished off.

RAT & MOUSE

Inspiration

In Japanese mythology, the rat is one of the most revered signs of the zodiac, and was often carved by early Japanese netsuke carvers. Sometimes they were carved in the form of a ball containing several rats, or as individuals gnawing through a rattan basket or eating the wax on a candle. A particular favourite was a baby rat scratching its ear. This was the very first netsuke I carved and the one which got me hooked on the subject.

Usually the rat is not held in the same high regard, so I modified the design to look more like a mouse. One of the main differences is that a rat's tail is segmented, whereas the tail of a mouse is not. I have carved several netsuke mice in boxwood, pear, apple and other woods as they have proved to be very popular.

Boxwood mouse

Dimensions (for both): Width: 1½in (38mm) Height: 1½in (38mm) Depth: 1½in (38mm)

Materials

• Boxwood, pear or applewood

• Buffalo horn for the eyes

Links

• Inlaying eyes (see pages 42–6)

• Carving short hair (see page 50)

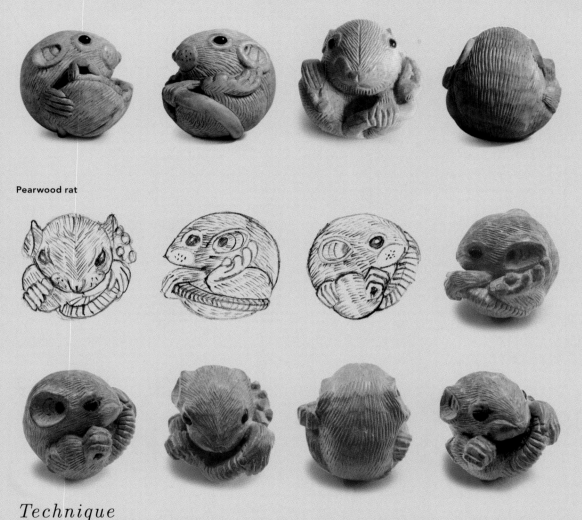

Pearwood rat

Technique

The drawings on these two pages show both the pearwood rat and the boxwood mouse. Their eyes were inlaid with buffalo horn.

They are a good exercise in carving short hair. Both pieces were waxed with a slightly darker polish to provide some contrast in the hair.

● Simple
● **Moderate**
● Advanced

CUTTLEFISH

Inspiration

The cuttlefish is another amazing creature. It is a fast swimmer and a good hunter with excellent eyesight. Cuttlefish can change their skin colour very quickly in order to blend into the background. Normally, they adopt a zebra-like skin pattern, which was a challenge to replicate on a netsuke carving. I drew detailed pictures of a cuttlefish from several angles in order to make an unusual and challenging carving.

Technique

I chose holly as its light colour contrasts with the dark markings. To achieve the striped effect I used a ¹⁄₁₆in (1.5mm) gouge to cut the pattern on its back, then filled it with hard black wax. The wax softens, fills the carved recesses, and hardens again when cool. I also marked the surface of the skirt around the outside of the cuttlefish's back and between its eyes with *ukibori* to leave a series of bumps. The eyes were inlaid with buffalo horn.

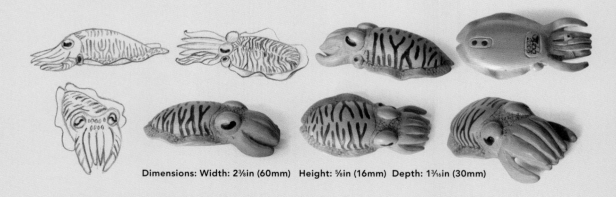

Dimensions: Width: 2⅜in (60mm)   Height: ⅝in (16mm)   Depth: 1³⁄₁₆in (30mm)

Materials

• Holly
• Buffalo horn for the eyes
• Black hard wax filler stick

Links

• *Ukibori* bumps (see pages 47–8)
• Hard wax inlay (see page 65)
• Inlaying eyes (see pages 42–6)
• Drilling cord holes (see page 69)

Simple ●
Moderate ●
Advanced ●

SNAIL

Inspiration

Most people do not like snails, but the early Japanese carvers created many netsuke snails, either on their own, on leaves, or on similar objects. I don't like the damage that snails do in my garden, but I still think that they are amazing creatures.

Technique

This piece is carved from a knot of Paraná pine from South America. Carving the parallel lines on the shell was very difficult to control as the wood is so hard. The design was developed to ensure that nothing broke off the snail. The body and eyes were wrapped round the shell, to indicate movement while keeping the piece compact.

Dimensions: Width: 2in (50mm) Height: 2in (50mm) Depth: 2in (50mm)

Materials

• Paraná pine, boxwood, pink ivory or tagua nut

Links

• Carving the shell (see page 53)
• Carving the body (see page 54)
• Drilling cord holes (see page 69)

Bactrian Camel

Inspiration

Camels are surprisingly large animals, with the ability to survive in harsh desert environments with very infrequent food and water. I once came across a double-hump Bactrian camel in northern China. When I saw a well-crafted resin-cast camel on a bric-a-brac stall it reminded me of this encounter.

I bought the piece with a view to recreating it in wood. The detail on the hair was very fine and I was interested to see whether this could be replicated as a miniature netsuke carving. The camel is resting on its folded legs and appears very much at peace, unlike many domesticated camels I have seen which are grumpy and sullen.

Dimensions: Width: 1⅞in (48mm) Height: 1³⁄₁₆in (30mm) Depth: ⅞in (22mm)

Materials

• Boxwood

• Imitation ivory and buffalo horn for the eyes

Links

• Inlaying eyes (see pages 42–6)

• Carving curly hair (see page 50)

• Drilling cord holes (see page 69)

Technique

I drew the outline onto a piece of boxwood, then cut out the profile of the camel and began to carve. Carving the slightly curly hair required firm control of a 1/16in (1.5mm) V-tool both at the beginning and at the end of each cut, in order to get the curves right. I stained the whole carving with coffee-coloured dye, lightly sanded it off and scraped the high spots. I added imitation ivory and buffalo-horn inserts to give definition to the camel's eyes.

Simple
Moderate
Advanced

BILLY GOAT

Inspiration

The goat is another sign of the Japanese zodiac and was often carved by traditional netsuke carvers in Japan. Goats were carved in all sorts of poses or in groups with young kids. I saw a braying billy goat in a book and decided to have a go at carving it, particularly as its long hair would be challenging to carve.

Technique

Since the hair is the most important aspect of this carving, I drew each individual hair in pencil, then used a 1/16in (1.5mm) V-tool to carve along the lines. I focused on small areas at a time, so that the pencil marks did not rub off. I inlaid the eyes with ivory and buffalo horn. There was no need to create cord holes since there were already natural openings between the legs of the goat.

Dimensions: Width: 1¾in (45mm) Height: 1¹¹⁄₁₆in (44mm) Depth: 1⁷⁄₃₂in (33mm)

Materials

• Boxwood

• Imitation ivory and buffalo horn for the eyes

Links

• Inlaying eyes (see pages 42–6)

• Carving long hair (see page 50)

MOLE

Inspiration

Some years ago, I had the chance to get a close look at a mole in my garden. It was beautiful with really smooth and sleek fur, with large front feet for digging. I played around with some sketches, before settling on the one shown here, with the mole curled up in a ball. Its legs and tail are held against its body so that nothing would break off during the carving.

Technique

I chose to carve the mole in African blackwood as it is more uniformly black than ebony. The wood was hard to carve, but it took on a superb polished finish closely resembling the smooth fur on a real mole. This piece would also carve well in buffalo horn as this is also very black and shines really nicely when polished. In order to achieve a very smooth finish, I went through the grades of sandpaper and then all the grades of Micro-Mesh, finishing with 12000 grit.

Dimensions: Width: 1¾in (45mm) Height: 2³⁄₁₆in (55mm) Depth: 1⁷⁄₁₆in (37mm)

Materials
• African blackwood, ebony or buffalo horn

Links
• Drilling cord holes (see page 69)

● Simple
● **Moderate**
● Advanced

HARE & TORTOISE

Inspiration

The hare and tortoise story is one of Aesop's well-known fables, where the slow and steady tortoise beats the fast hare in a race. My aim was to make the tortoise appear smug while the hare wore a frustrated look with angry eyes. I placed the finishing tape under the chin of the tortoise to signify that he is the winner.

Again I decided to carve it in boxwood for its ability to take high detail. The grain of the wood runs along the length of the hare to ensure that the legs would not break off and that the hare would stay firmly on the tortoise's shell.

Dimensions: Width: 3in (75mm) Height: 2³⁄₁₆in (55mm) Depth: 1⁹⁄₁₆in (40mm)

Materials

• Boxwood
• Imitation ivory and buffalo horn for eyes
• Dark wax polish

Links

• Carving short hair (see page 50)
• Carving bumps (see pages 47–8)
• Inlaying eyes (see pages 42–6)
• Sparrow pecking (see page 49)

Technique

I carved the bumps individually on the body of the tortoise and, after clearing out between them, I sparrow-pecked the gaps. The shell was divided into platelets, with each one carved using a 1/16in (1.5mm) V-tool to create the growth rings. For the hair I used the same tool to create several short cuts with an overall smooth appearance. The eyes for both animals were inlaid with ivory and buffalo horn. The whole netsuke was waxed with a darker wax to lie in the low spots and to enhance the detail.

● Simple
● **Moderate**
● Advanced

HORSE

Inspiration

I bought a beautiful little ivory netsuke horse many years ago while working in Hong Kong – before the sale of ivory was banned. Whilst strolling around the streets on Hong Kong Island one evening, I noticed a tiny sign among thousands of others advertising ivory carvings and netsuke.

Inside, the only netsuke on sale was a small horse. When I saw it, I just had to buy it as it was so full of charm and character. Although I had a real netsuke to copy, I also drew the little horse out, to provide me with a better picture of what it would look like from every angle.

Dimensions: Width: 1⁷⁄₁₆in (36mm) Height: 1¼in (32mm) Depth: ¹⁵⁄₁₆in (25mm)

Materials

- Huon pine, boxwood, holly or other woods
- Imitation ivory and buffalo horn for the eyes

Links

- Inlaying eyes (see pages 42–6)
- Drilling cord holes (see page 69)

Technique

Like many netsuke, the horse looks deceptively simple to carve. The secret to successfully reproducing one is to get all the proportions right. Keep checking the dimensions throughout the process. You may need to redraw some parts to ensure that everything is in the right place. I carved the piece in Huon pine and inlaid the eyes with imitation ivory and buffalo horn.

● Simple
● **Moderate**
● Advanced

TOAD

Inspiration

Many people think toads and frogs are ugly, but in my opinion they are full of character, as well as a delight to carve. I have carved many full-sized ones and several netsuke toads in a wide range of materials including boxwood, ivory and malachite. This particular toad is a natterjack which has a ridge down the middle of its back. Other types of toad do not have this feature.

Technique

The toad was carved from boxwood with eyes inlaid with imitation ivory and buffalo horn. You could also use coloured resins or other coloured woods to create the eyes. I sparrow-pecked around the bumps, then finished the carvings with a relatively dark wax. The wax lies in the sparrow-pecked holes and makes the bumps stand out better.

Dimensions: Width: 2⅜in (60mm) Height: 1⅜in (35mm) Depth: 1⁹⁄₁₆in (40mm)

Materials

• Boxwood, but could use many other woods

• Imitation ivory and buffalo horn for the eyes

Links

• Carving bumps (see pages 47–8)

• Sparrow-pecking (see page 49)

• Inlaying eyes (see pages 42–6)

• Colouring (see pages 62–6)

Ox

Inspiration

The ox is another sign of the zodiac, commonly carved in Japan. The animal was much valued as it was traditionally used to pull the plough. Although it is very strong, it is also easy to control because of its gentle nature. I wanted to carve one at rest, to show both its gentleness and its strength.

Technique

First, I made several sketches until I was happy that I had captured the contradiction between the strength of the ox and its gentleness. I then set about carving it in boxwood. When it was finished I dyed it a coffee colour, before sanding off the high spots so that they contrasted with the darker low spots.

Dimensions: Width 2⁵⁄₁₆in (58mm) Height 1³⁄₁₆in (30mm) Depth 1³⁄₁₆in (30mm)

Materials

- Boxwood
- Imitation ivory and buffalo horn for the eyes

Links

- Inlaying eyes (see pages 42–6)
- Carving hair (see page 50)

● Simple
● Moderate
● **Advanced**

TORTOISE

Inspiration

I have carved a number of full-sized tortoises, before I decided to carve a miniature one with a difference. This piece is on the upper limit of the size for a netsuke.

Technique

I used small pieces of dark laburnum wood to inlay the shell. The shape of each segment was drawn onto the shell before being carved. Each recess was drilled and carved into the shape of the segment. The pieces of laburnum were shaped individually until they fitted tightly into the appropriate recess. After gluing in the laburnum, I rounded off the surface of each piece. Finally, the eyes were inlaid with imitation ivory and buffalo horn.

Dimensions: Width: 2¾in (70mm) Height: 1⁹⁄₁₆in (40mm) Depth: 1¹¹⁄₁₆in (43mm)

Materials

• Boxwood

• Laburnum or walnut for inlaying shell

• Imitation ivory and buffalo horn for the eyes

Links

• Inlaying eyes (see pages 55–7)

• Sparrow-pecking (see page 49)

• Drilling cord holes (see page 69)

CARP

Inspiration

In my youth I would often go fishing for carp, and came to respect their cunning and strength. I once fished throughout the night and was catapulted from near sleep to near heart attack in a split second when a decent-sized fish took the bait unexpectedly. The Japanese also have great admiration for carp, demonstrated by the large number of them which occur in Japanese art, including netsuke. I chose to carve a mirror carp based on the design of a classical netsuke with its tail curved round to join the pectoral fin. To enhance the carving I gilded the scales.

Technique

To make the eyes come alive, I drilled the eye sockets, gilded them, and put in small amber dowels. I drilled the back of the amber and placed black ink in the holes for the pupils. The polished amber eyes glow when the light catches them. They were difficult to make as they were so small, and took several attempts to get right. This typifies netsuke carving: the end result should be as good as possible regardless of the time it takes. The natural opening between the tail and the pectoral fin was large enough for the cord, so I did not drill any cord holes.

Dimensions: Width: 2³⁄₁₆in (55mm) Height: 1⁹⁄₁₆in (40mm) Depth: 1¾in (45mm)

Materials

• Boxwood
• Amber for the eyes, but could use imitation ivory and buffalo horn
• Gilding varnish for the scales

Links

• Carving scales (see page 51)
• Inlaying eyes (see pages 42–6)
• Gilding (see page 66)

DRAGON

Inspiration

Japanese mythology with stories about dragons, and other strange creatures that were frequently carved by the early netsuke carvers. This particular netsuke is one of my own designs. While on a business trip to New Zealand, I picked up a few books on bone and jade carving. One particular shape caught my interest and became the initial starting point for my design.

I began experimenting with the shape, adding a head and feet to create my New Zealand blue dragon. On the trip, I also bought a couple of paua shells and decided to use this shell to inlay the dragon and to add colour.

My original sketch of a jade

The dragon doodles developed from the sketch.

Dimensions: Width: 2⁹/₁₆in (65mm) Height: 2in (50mm) Depth: 1½in (38mm)

Materials

• Boxwood

• Paua shell, resin veneer or wood veneer

• Imitation ivory and buffalo horn for the eyes

Links

• Inlaying eyes (see pages 42–6)

• Inlaying paua shell, resin or wood veneer
  see pages 55–7)

Technique

I carved the dragon in boxwood, inlaying the eyes with ivory and buffalo horn. Cutting and inlaying the paua shell around the curved body involved cutting the shell into segments and gluing them into a carved recess. I then cut and shaped the shell with a small cutter held in my multi-tool. Firm control was needed to prevent the cutter from skidding across the surface. Cutting the scale segments so that each fitted snugly against the next was time-consuming, but it is very important not to rush your carving. If you prefer, the scales can be inlaid using different colour wood veneers, mother of pearl, or coloured resin; cut thinly and shaped to fit.

● Simple
● Moderate
● **Advanced**

PENGUINS

Inspiration

While watching a wildlife film about penguins I was amazed to see how quick and agile they were under water. I imagined them hunting in a group after a shoal of fish and made a few sketches of rockhopper penguins turning at speed and swimming under the water after a shoal of small fish. The Japanese have a way of suggesting the movement of water in their carvings, which I wanted to incorporate. In the photographs you can see how the water effect is used successfully and how it holds much of the carving together, in that the shoal of fishes at the front and the wings and feet of the penguins towards the back are both attached to it.

Dimensions: Width: 2⁹/₁₆in (65mm) Height: 2in (50mm) Depth: 1½in (38mm)

Materials

• Boxwood

• Imitation ivory and buffalo horn for the eyes

• Various dyes

Links

• Inlaying eyes (see pages 42–6)

• Feathering (see page 52)

• Drilling cord holes (see page 69)

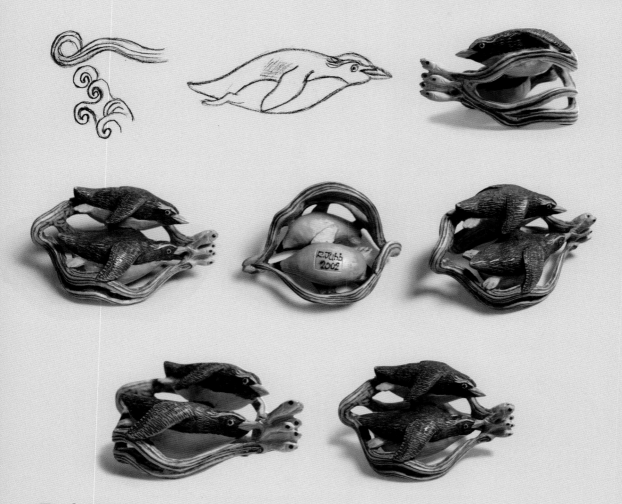

Technique

This is a more advanced netsuke carving, again created from boxwood as this allowed me to carve the effect of the water without breaking the wood. I made very short cuts with a ¹⁄₁₆in (1.5mm) V-tool to gain the right effect for the penguins' stiff yet waterproof feathers.

The eyes of the penguins were inlaid with ivory and buffalo horn and the fishes were inlaid with buffalo horn. The penguins' beaks and feet were dyed pink, the upper part of their bodies black, and the grooves in the water were dyed blue.

● Simple
● Moderate
● **Advanced**

Octopus

Inspiration

Octopus are highly intelligent creatures who use stealth and camouflage to catch their prey. The blue-ringed octopus in Australia simply amazed me. It is among the smallest of all the octopus family, yet it is also one of the most deadly creatures. The blue rings appear when the octopus is angry and about to attack.

Early Japanese carvers also admired octopus and would often carve them as netsuke pieces, sometimes embracing a pearl-diving woman. I decided to try my hand at carving a blue-ringed octopus and inlaying it with blue resin. When this is held in the right light it produces striking, blue ring effects.

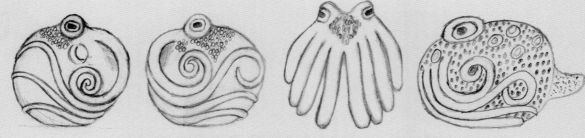

Dimensions: Width: 1⁹⁄₁₆in (40mm) Height: 1³⁄₈in (35mm) Depth: 1³⁄₈in (35mm)

Materials

• Boxwood or holly
• Imitation ivory and buffalo horn for the eyes
• Blue resin

Links

• Inlaying eyes (see pages 42–6)
• Inlaying (see pages 55–7)
• *Ukibori* bumps (see page 48–9)
• Drilling cord holes (see page 69)

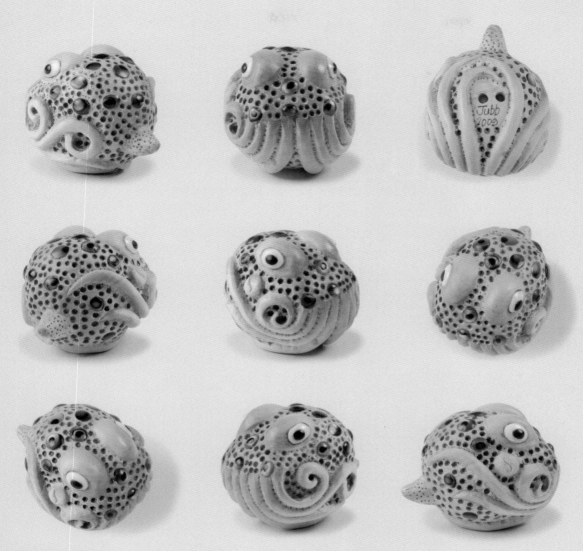

Technique

I used the *ukibori* technique to create bumps in front of the eyes on the common octopus. I inlaid the blue-ringed octopus with blue resin dowels, rounding these off to little domes. I drilled all over the surface of the netsuke with a small-diameter drill to a shallow depth to provide a different texture to the surface, as can be seen in the photographs above. Also note the curious point on the body of the blue-ringed octopus.

Penguins (page 146)

Toadstools (page 122)

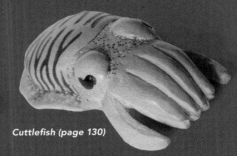

Cuttlefish (page 130)

TO SCALE

Due to the many images included within the author's collection, it was not possible to include all the netsuke on these pages at full size. With this in mind, this spread includes a picture of each netsuke to scale to assist you when you are creating your own carving.

Horse (page 138)

Platypus (page 126)

Dormouse (page 120)

Carp (page 143)

Mole (page 134)

Bactrian Camel (page 132)

Toad (page 140)

Mouse (page 128)

Rabbit (page 125)

Dragon (page 144)

Bumblebee (page 123)

Nautilus (page 124)

Rat (page 128)

Snail (page 131)

Tortoise (page 142)

Owl (page 119)

Billy Goat (page 133)

Ox (page 141)

Octopus (page 148)

Hedgehog (page 121)

Hare & Tortoise (page 136)

GALLERY

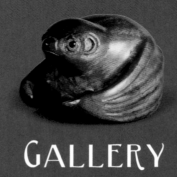

GALLERY

The aim of this chapter to show just a small sample of the amazing range of subjects which can be carved as netsuke, and hopefully to inspire you to have a go yourself. It includes netsuke pieces in my own collection, some which I have carved and others that I have purchased, as well as netsuke owned by friends who have kindly agreed to their being photographed and included in this book.

Netsuke from my own personal collection.

A netsuke rat bought in Hong Kong (possibly made from ironwood).

A netsuke hare from Hong Kong (possibly made from ironwood).

A netsuke toad purchased in Hong Kong (unknown material).

Netsuke snail carved in boxwood.

A modern netsuke pig in boxwood given to me by a close friend.

One of my earliest netsuke carvings of a tortoise in boxwood.

This snake encoiling a toad is based on a traditional Japanese netsuke and is carved in boxwood. The snake is a small python with its eyes inlaid with paua shell. The toad's eyes are inlaid with ivory and buffalo horn.

I found this netsuke in a local flea market for a modest sum. The mouse is sitting on a rattan basket with a baby mouse sticking his nose out the other end. It is made from boxwood and has been stained.

I carved this pair of badger cubs in holly inlaid with African blackwood. I inlaid the whites around the eyes and the ears with holly and inserted buffalo-horn eyes. I used grey wax to make it appear more realistic.

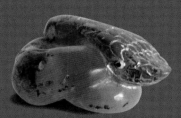

After carving this amber snake, I tried to gild it, but without success. However, it feels nice to hold and still worth keeping.

I bought this netsuke cat from a bric-a-brac stall. At first I thought it was made from amber, but it turned out to be resin.

This mother toad has three babies on her back. This is a resin casting, but the underside has been hand-carved and stained.

This is another of my favourite toads. It is carved in malachite which is very hard and difficult to work, but I love the grain.

This tiger was the first ivory netsuke I carved. A tiger scratching its ear is a much-carved Japanese netsuke subject.

This boxwood dragon is inlaid with paua shell and gilded. The eyes are inlaid with ivory and buffalo horn.

Dorothy Wilson's Collection

The photographs on the next few pages are all from Dorothy's collection. I have tried to group them together where there are similarities, and added comments along the way.

This monkey is trying to pick up a tortoise, which can be better seen from underneath. It is difficult to determine what the material is, although it could be bone.

From above this netsuke looks like a tortoise. However, when it is turned upside down it becomes a bearded man. It is made from wood and signed near the tassel on the man.

This camel has its front legs resting on a tortoise. It is carved in ivory.

This netsuke could either be a goat, or a ram, either way it seems very contented. Its eyes are inlaid with a green stone.

A pair of ducks rummaging through the leaves on a pond makes a delightful carving with movement and character.

The three wise monkeys, 'see no evil, speak no evil and hear no evil', all joined together. The carving is possibly ivory, with very fine hair.

This rabbit appears to have been made from bone with startling red eyes. It is finely carved all over with hair, but since it has not been inked in, it is very difficult to see.

The mouse has eaten its way into the side of a rattan bag to get at its contents, then eaten its way out of the other end.

Tagua nut was used for this walrus, full of character.

These netsuke from the animal kingdom have all been carved in ivory. Elephants don't appear very often in netsuke carving, but the cockerel, wild boar and horse are frequently carved.

The elephant has a rat or a mouse on its back; presumably that is why it is trumpeting with indignation.

The feathers on this cockerel are quite deep and very effective.

I like the composition of this netsuke horse, as it makes it look charming.

This is a resting wild boar complete with tusks and a long mane behind its head.

The following netsuke are made from tagua nut. They are all modern designs, although tagua nuts were carved by the Japanese well over a hundred years ago. Their yellowish colour suggests that these pieces have all been stained.

This shiny tagua-nut crab shows what effect a good polish can achieve. Its eyes are inlaid with buffalo horn.

These two charming little figures were bought together in China.

This group of three baby rabbits are on a partly carved tagua nut. The bottom half has been left as a natural nut including the skin.

These netsuke show characters which feature frequently in Japanese mythology.

The seven gods of fortune.
This group seems to be made from resin, possibly cast from an ivory carving with amazing detail.

Toad sennin.
Sennins are magical creatures, a bit like spirits. This pair are made from deer antler, probably by the same carver.

These next few netsuke show people carrying out various activities, either as their trade or depicting a story from Japanese mythology.

The faces and the decorative clothing on the first two figures are so alike that they are very likely to have been created by the same carver.

This man is carrying a bunch of flowers either for his wife or for selling on the street. It is finely carved in ivory with lots of detail.

The basket of fruit that this man is carrying indicates that he is a fruit seller. The netsuke is carved in ivory.

This man is expecting a good night out. He has a pipe for a relaxing smoke, a dice for gambling and a picture of his young lady depicted on his sleeve.

These three netsuke figures are all made from resin.

This sleeping man is likely to be having a nightmare, indicated by the demon by his side which is sticking his tongue right out. There is probably a Japanese story to go with this.

This figure has a serene face and is holding something tight in both hands.

Here we have a scholar who has fallen asleep over his desk and is enjoying his slumber, shown by the smile on his face.

The following four figures are carved from ivory.

I think the expression on this washerwoman's face is wonderful; she is obviously happy in her work.

I can't make up my mind whether this man is eating a meal from his bowl or begging.

The fisherman is looking very pleased with his catch.

This man is holding a gourd in one hand and has an animal suspended from the other, indicating that he is going home to cook.

The two following netsuke are Japanese mythical dragons.

This dragon is carved in a ball. It is made from ebony, with eyes inlaid with buffalo horn. A small cartouche carries the carver's signature.

This time the dragon is a modern carving in boxwood that has been stained. He looks a fierce beast with a body that twists and turns, ending with a fan-like tail.

Below are photographs of carved *ojime*, the beads which tighten the cord from the netsuke to the *inro*. These are usually very small and carved into all kinds of miniature and intricate subjects.

They are carved from the same materials as netsuke, as well as pips and nuts. As far as I can tell, one *ojime* is the shell of a nut as the nut is still inside, while the others could be made from nuts, pips or wood.

This ojime is made from the shell of a nut and is the largest one shown. There are 18 miniscule figures carved onto the surface, as well as flowers and several other objects.

All ojime have a hole right through, from the top to the bottom, although it cannot be seen from this angle.

The ojime shown above is an intricate carving of a water buffalo.

This ojime has a horse and three figures carved round its circumference.

The netsuke here are two very different Buddhas, a *kirin* (similiar to a unicorn in Japanese mythology), and a *shishi* (a mythical lion often seen playing with a ball).

Here is the smallest Buddha carved in ivory. He looks very relaxed and happy.

This ivory Buddha is much larger. He also looks very happy, even if a little overweight.

This is how most kirin netsuke appear, seated with its head pointing upwards.

This shishi netsuke is likely to have been made from bone as no ivory grain can be detected.

These netsuke are commonly referred to as clam netsuke, although the first one looks more like a cockle shell, and the second one a mussel. They are usually carved with the shell partly open to show the scene inside.

This scene, carved in ivory, shows trees and buildings, alongside a small boat with its sail up, minute figures, as well as two ducks with their ducklings.

Here three figures are shown in the foreground with trees behind them. There is a snail carved on the upper shell.

Paul Reader's Collection
The following netsuke are all modern wooden netsuke carvings purchased by Paul Reader.

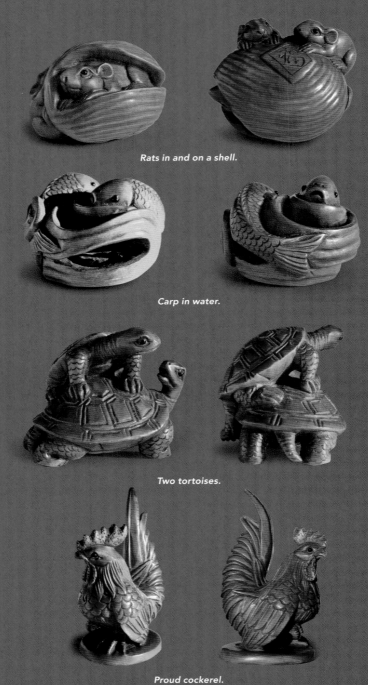

Rats in and on a shell.

Carp in water.

Two tortoises.

Proud cockerel.

Work by professional netsuke carver Sue Wraight

I have saved the best until last. I mentioned earlier in this book how Sue Wraight's work inspired me to first start carving netsuke.

Sue is one of just a few professional women netsuke carvers in the world, in an art form traditionally dominated by men. One of her netsuke pieces was commissioned by the Government of Victoria as the State's gift to former President George Bush senior during his visit to Australia in 1992.

Sue has also sold a number of pieces to a Japanese royal, which is one of the highest accolades a netsuke carver can achieve.

I have included photographs of her fantastic work to show just what can be achieved with original ideas, an eye for design, experience and great skill. Some of the outstanding features of Sue's work are the brilliant ideas that she translates into amazingly detailed netsuke sculptures.

Frog on a Taro Leaf – boxwood with amber eyes.

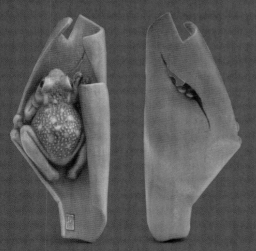

Frog on Bark (front and rear views).

Fighting in Flight – boxwood with horn eyes.

The netsuke below are from Sue's work shown at the International Netsuke Society Convention, Boston, 2001.

Her attention to detail and the quality of the carvings is amazing and leaves me very envious of her skills.

Cicada – stained boxwood.

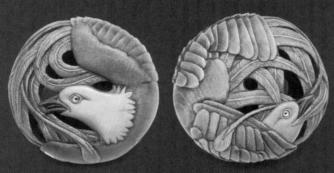

Paradise Courtship (birds of paradise), front and back – stained boxwood.

The Goose that Laid the Golden Egg – bleached boxwood and amber.

The Happy Angler – stained boxwood.

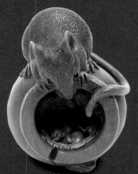

Awakening – boxwood. This dormouse has
been woken from hibernation by the ladybird
which is tickling the side of its head.

Mouse on a Barrel – boxwood.
Its babies are inside the barrel.

Coral Basket – tagua nut and boxwood with various inlays.
The group of sea creatures fits into the coral basket.

The Fox and the Mask from Aesop's Fables – meaning that
the outside show is no substitute for inner worth.

BIBLIOGRAPHY

Bandini. R., *Expressions of Style – Netsuke as Art*, Scholten Japanese Art, 2001

Benson, P., *The Art of Carving Netsuke*, GMC publications Ltd, 2010

Bushell, R., *An Introduction to Netsuke: (V & A Museum Introductions to the Decorative Arts)*, Stemmer House Publishers Inc, 1982

Bushell, R. & Masotoshi, N., *The Art of Netsuke Carving*, Weatherhill Inc, 1992

Bushell, R., *The Wonderful World of Netsuke*, Tuttle Publishing, 1995

Cohen, G., *In Search of Netsuke and Inro*, Luzac & Company, 1974

Earle, J., *An Introduction to Netsuke*, Her Majesty's Stationery Office, 1982

Earle, J., *Netsuke: Fantasy and Reality in Japanese Miniature Sculpture*, Museum of Fine Arts Boston, 2004

Hutt, J., *Japanese Netsuke*, Victoria and Albert Museum Far Eastern series, 2003

Kinsey, M., *Contemporary Netsuke*, Tuttle Publishing, 1977

Miriam, K., *Living Masters of Netsuke*, Kodansha America, 1984

Putney, C. M., *Japanese Treasures – The Art of Netsuke Carving*, The Toledo Museum of Art, 2000

Sandfield, N., Shelton, H., Ichiro: *Master Netsuke Carver*, Shelton Family Press, 2009

Symmes, Jr. E., Netsuke: *Japanese Life and Legend in Miniature*, Tuttle Publishing, 2000

Veleanu, M., *Netsuke*, Schiffer Publishing Ltd, 2008

Other sources include:
MUSEUMS – especially the British Museum or the Victoria and Albert Museum, London.

ANTIQUE DEALER'S CATALOGUES – such as Sotheby's, Phillips' and Christie's auction houses.

THE INTERNET – International Netsuke Society (www.netsuke.org); – Netsuke & Japanese Art Online Research Centre (www.netsukeonline.org).

SUPPLIERS

WOODCARVING TOOLS

Tilgear
(Dockyard Micro Carving
and Powergrip tools)
 + 44 (0) 808 168 1800
www.tilgear.info

Axminster Tool Centre
+ 44 (0) 800 371 822
www.axminster.co.uk

Woodcraft
1-800-225-1153
www.woodcraft.com

Pfeil tools
+41 (0) 62 922 45 65
www.pfeiltools.ch

Henry Taylor tools
+ 44 (0) 114 234 0282
www.henrytaylortools.co.uk

Ashley Iles tools
+ 44 (0) 1790 763372
www.ashleyiles.co.uk

Robert Sorby tools
+ 44 (0) 114 225 0700
 www.robert-sorby.co.uk

Ramelson tools
+1 (973) 589-5422
www.ramelson.com

Perma-grit tools
+ 44 (0) 1529 455 034
www.permagrit.com

POWER TOOLS & CUTTERS

Foredom
+1 (203) 792-8622
www.foredom.com

Dremel
+ 44 (0) 844 7360107
1-800-437-3635
www.dremel.com

Saburr-tooth
+1 (586) 731-0990
www.saburr-tooth.com

MATERIALS
Amber, copal, paua shell,
malachite and soapstone can
all be purchased from fossil
or stone shops.

TIMBER

Timberline of Tonbridge
+ 44 (0) 1732 355 626
www.exotichardwoods.co.uk

Yandles
+ 44 (0) 1935 822 207
www.yandles.co.uk

W.L. West & Sons Ltd
+ 44 (0) 1798 861 611
www.wlwest.co.uk

WAXES, POLISHES & DYES

Liberon
+ 44 (0) 1797 367 555
www.liberon.co.uk

Rustins
+ 44 (0) 20 8450 4666
www.rustins.co.uk

Picreator
(Rennaisance wax)
+ 44 (0) 208 202 8972
www.picreator.co.uk

Dylon
+ 44 (0) 1737 742 020
www.dylon.co.uk

GLOSSARY

Amber Fossilized pine tree resin, with colour varying from milky white to clear honey and semi-transparent.

Buffalo horn From the water buffalo – jet black in colour.

Copal Newly harvested pine resin, like amber but not so hard.

Hako Small box netsuke.

Himotoshi Holes in a netsuke to take the cord.

Ichiraku Gourd shaped netsuke from woven bamboo.

Inro A tiered box for seals and medicine hung by a cord and kept in place by a netsuke.

Kagami & kagamibuta Netsuke of a small bowl into which a metal disc fits like a mirror.

Katabori Carving in the round, with every surface carved, including underneath.

Kebori Hairline engraving.

Kimono Japanese traditional clothing.

Kirin A mythological animal – thought of as similar to a unicorn.

Kurumikli A hollow and perforated netsuke-like figures in a clam shell.

Manju A round and flat netsuke named after the manju bun, which it resembles.

Malachite A hard green stone containing copper and suitable for carving.

Marubori Three-dimensional carvings.

Mask netsuke Miniature versions of masks used in traditional Japanese theatre.

Mother of pearl Sea shell with the surface ground off to reveal a shiny silvery surface.

Multi-tool A rotary hand-held power tool which holds drills and cutters.

Netsuke A carved toggle designed to hold the *inro* in place when suspended from the *obi*.

Netsuke-shi Japanese netsuke carvers.

Obi The sash worn around a Japanese kimono.

Ojime A bead to tighten the cord above an *inro*.

Okimono Fine carving larger than a netsuke which are placed on a shelf to be viewed.

Oriental signs of the zodiac Animals used in Japan to represent the signs of the zodiac.

Paua shell Abalone shell with the surface ground off to reveal lovely blue/green colours.

Resins These can imitate various shells, marble, ivory etc., available in sheets or sticks.

Ryusa Perforated round netsuke like a *manju*.

Sagemono A word for all items that are suspended from the sash or *obi*.

Sashi An elongated netsuke that is tucked into the top of the *obi*.

Sennin Immortal people associated with different mythological subjects.

Shishi Mythological lion often shown with front paw(s) resting on a ball.

Shikakemono Trick netsuke with hidden movable parts which move remote parts, such as protruding tongues and eyes.

Soapstone Naturally occurring volcanic dust compressed over millions of years into stone which can vary in hardness.

Tagua nut A South American nut which is white and very hard, known sometimes in English as vegetable ivory, and in Japanese as *bunroji*.

Ukibori A method of making small bumps on the surface of a netsuke.

Umimatsu Fossilized coral used for carving or decoration.

V-tool A tool which cuts a V section into the wood, particularly useful for hair or fur.

About the Author

Bob Jubb has been woodcarving since the late 1960s, yet it wasn't until he came across professional carver Sue Wraight's exquisite pieces that he began to carve Japanese netsuke. Once Bob had carved his first piece, a baby rat – a classical and much carved Japanese subject – he was hooked.

Since then, his collection has steadily grown in size. Although his netsuke pieces are in high demand, with commissions coming from Australia, New Zealand and South Africa as well as the UK, Bob always keeps the first of any new netsuke that he carves.

He has also won several awards at the London Woodworking show and the Sussex Woodcraft Society Annual Exhibition, including best in show (four times), first place for miniature carvings (ten times), and a range of gold, silver and bronze medals. He is also a founder member of the Sussex Woodcraft Society, which has a membership of around 140 woodworkers.

INDEX

To place an order or to request a catalogue, contact:

GMC Publications Ltd

Castle Place, 166 High Street, Lewes, East Sussex, BN7 1XU, United Kingdom

Tel: +44 (0)1273 488005   Fax: +44 (0)1273 402866 www.gmcbooks.com